A WHO HQ GRAPHIC NOVEL

Who Was Ra... e the Queen o...?

MARIE ANTOINETTE

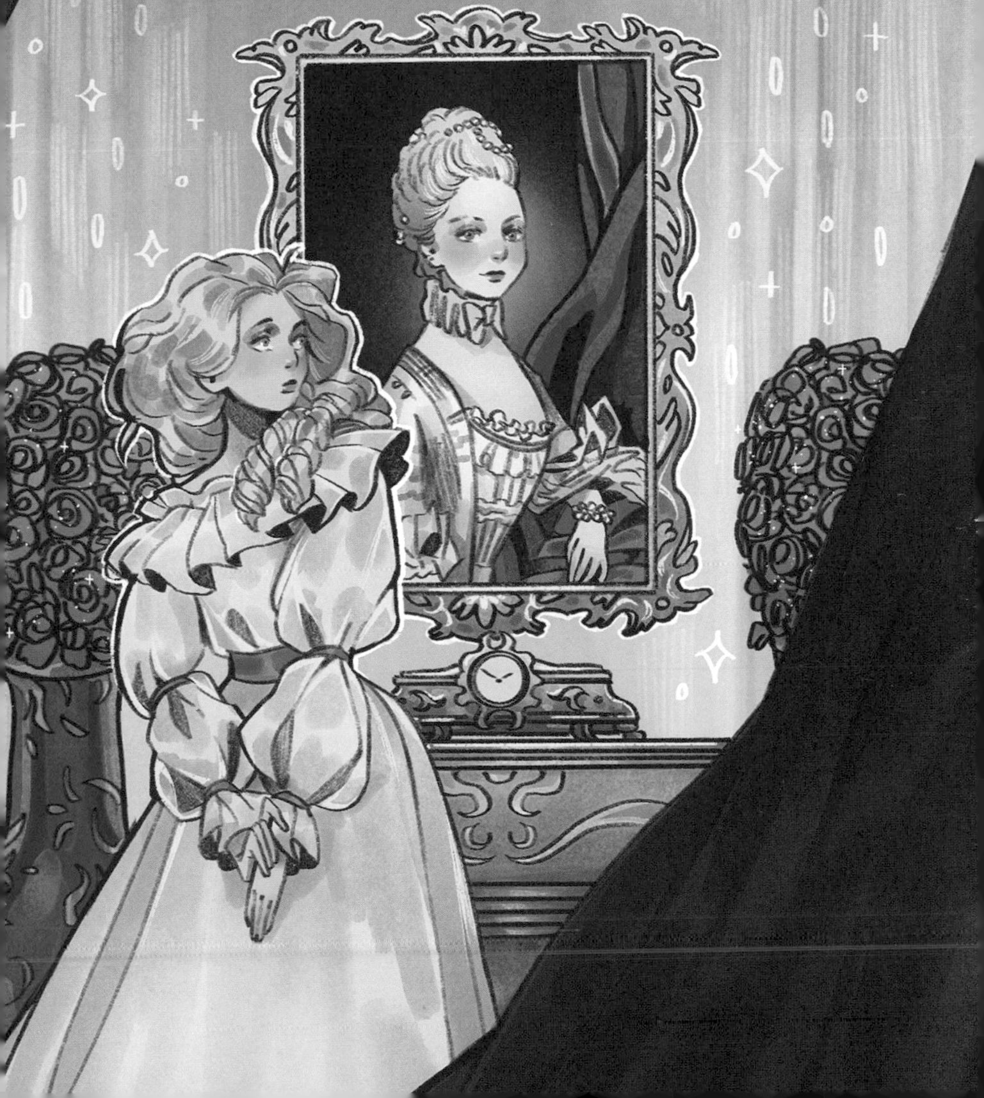

Dedicated to my friend Brinson
who inspired my fascination with Marie Antoinette.
And a special thanks to my editors Rachel and Celina—BL

Dedicated to Stephanie Cooke, Bianca Siercke,
and my agent Maria Vicente. Thank you for helping me
get my foot in the door. I owe you the world—RR

PENGUIN WORKSHOP
An imprint of Penguin Random House LLC, New York

First published in the United States of America by Penguin Workshop,
an imprint of Penguin Random House LLC, New York, 2024

Visit us online at penguinrandomhouse.com.

Library of Congress Cataloging-in-Publication Data is available.

Manufactured in China

ISBN 9780593385555 (pbk)   10 9 8 7 6 5 4 3 2 1 TOPL
ISBN 9780593385548 (hc)   10 9 8 7 6 5 4 3 2 1 TOPL

Lettering by Comicraft
Design by Jay Emmanuel

This is a work of nonfiction. All of the events that unfold in the narrative are rooted
in or inspired by historical fact. Some dialogue and characters have been fictionalized
in order to illustrate or teach a historical point. Some settings and timelines have
been changed in service of the narrative.

For more information about your favorite historical figures, places, and events,
please visit whohq.com.

A WHO HQ GRAPHIC NOVEL

Who Was Raised to Be the Queen of France?

MARIE ANTOINETTE

by Bones Leopard
illustrated by Robin Richardson

Penguin Workshop

Introduction

Before becoming the queen of France, Marie Antoinette was known by a different name: Maria Antonia, or simply "Antoine" to her family. She was the fifteenth child born to the Habsburg line under Holy Roman Empress Maria Theresa, who ruled over much of western and central Europe, including what is now Austria and Hungary. No one expected Maria Antonia to have an important marriage anytime soon, so during her childhood the attention went to her older sisters. With this free rein, she would skip lessons and pull pranks on tutors and other nobles.

Before the age of thirteen, Maria Antonia could not read or write very well in any language expected of royalty, such as Italian, English, and French, but she was fluent in speaking German, her native tongue. While Maria Antonia was beautiful and talented in the arts—especially the harp, harpsichord, and flute—Maria Theresa was disappointed to see such a gap in her daughter's abilities.

At the time, the Holy Roman Empire and many countries in Europe were coming out of the Seven Years' War, which is considered the first global conflict in modern history. In 1768, as a way to cement the relatively new alliance between the

French and Habsburg thrones, Maria Theresa set her sights on securing a marriage between Maria Antonia and the future king Louis XVI of France, called Louis Auguste. To educate Maria Antonia for her new role, Mathieu Jacques de Vermond arrived at Schönbrunn Palace, one of the Habsburgs' main residences. But Maria Antonia, still young and playful at age thirteen, had a lot of work ahead of her to prepare for French society.

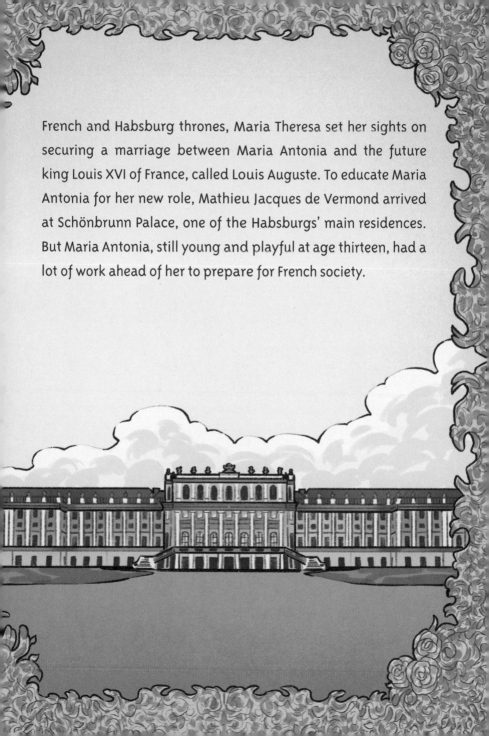

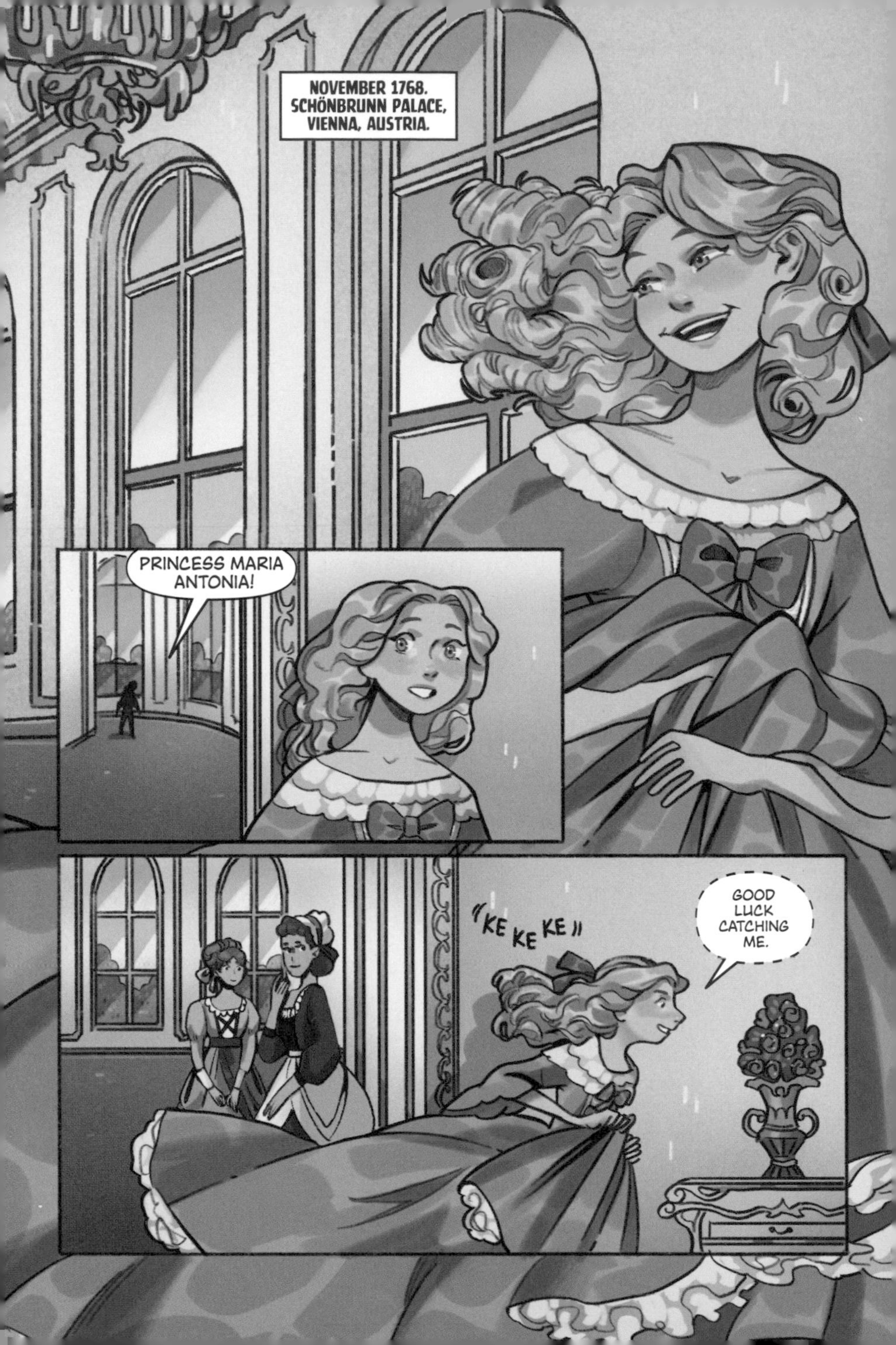
NOVEMBER 1768. SCHÖNBRUNN PALACE, VIENNA, AUSTRIA.
PRINCESS MARIA ANTONIA!
"KE KE KE"
GOOD LUCK CATCHING ME.

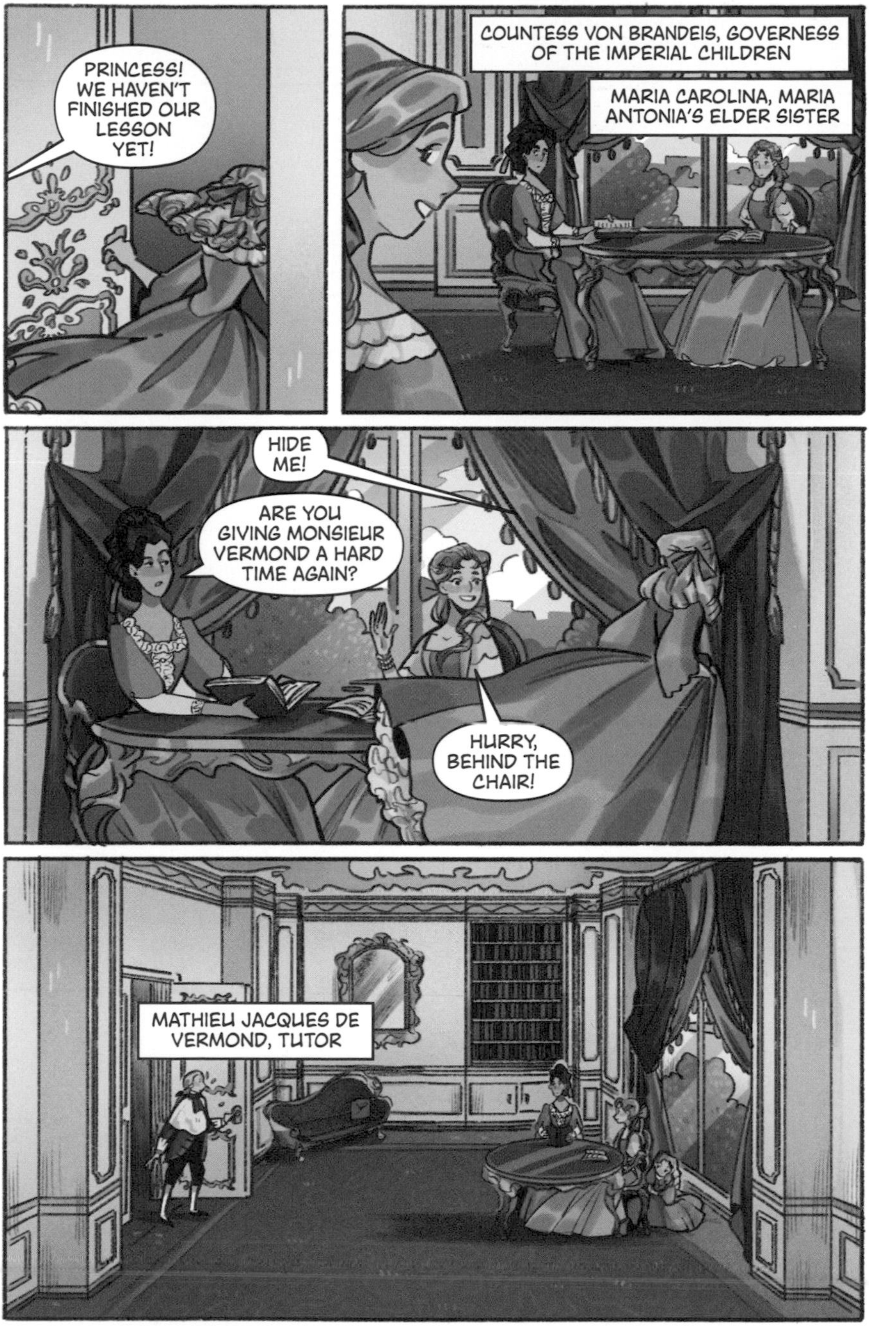
PRINCESS! WE HAVEN'T FINISHED OUR LESSON YET!
COUNTESS VON BRANDEIS, GOVERNESS OF THE IMPERIAL CHILDREN
MARIA CAROLINA, MARIA ANTONIA'S ELDER SISTER
HIDE ME!
ARE YOU GIVING MONSIEUR VERMOND A HARD TIME AGAIN?
HURRY, BEHIND THE CHAIR!
MATHIEU JACQUES DE VERMOND, TUTOR

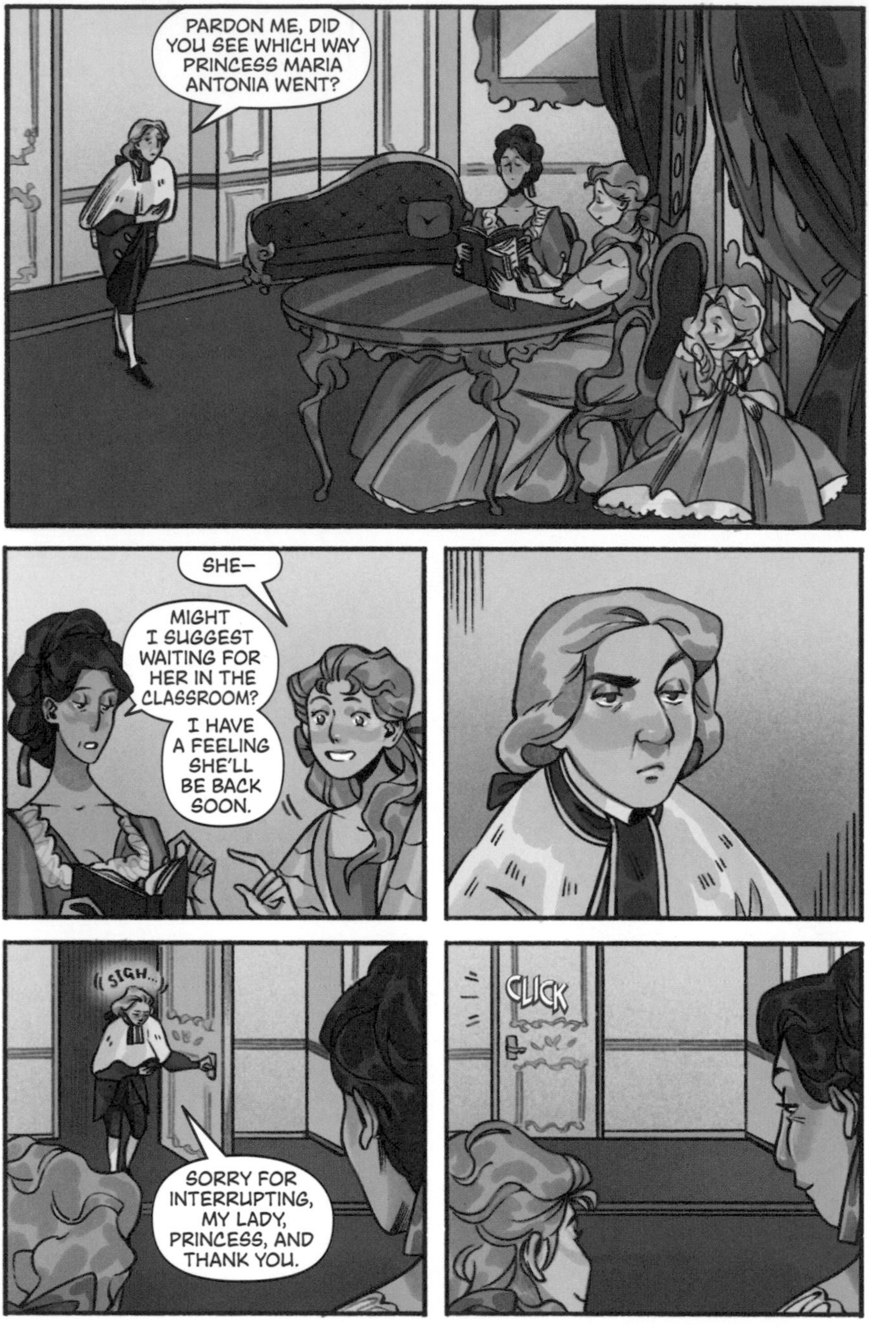
PARDON ME, DID YOU SEE WHICH WAY PRINCESS MARIA ANTONIA WENT?
SHE—
MIGHT I SUGGEST WAITING FOR HER IN THE CLASSROOM?
I HAVE A FEELING SHE'LL BE BACK SOON.
SIGH...
SORRY FOR INTERRUPTING, MY LADY, PRINCESS, AND THANK YOU.
CLICK

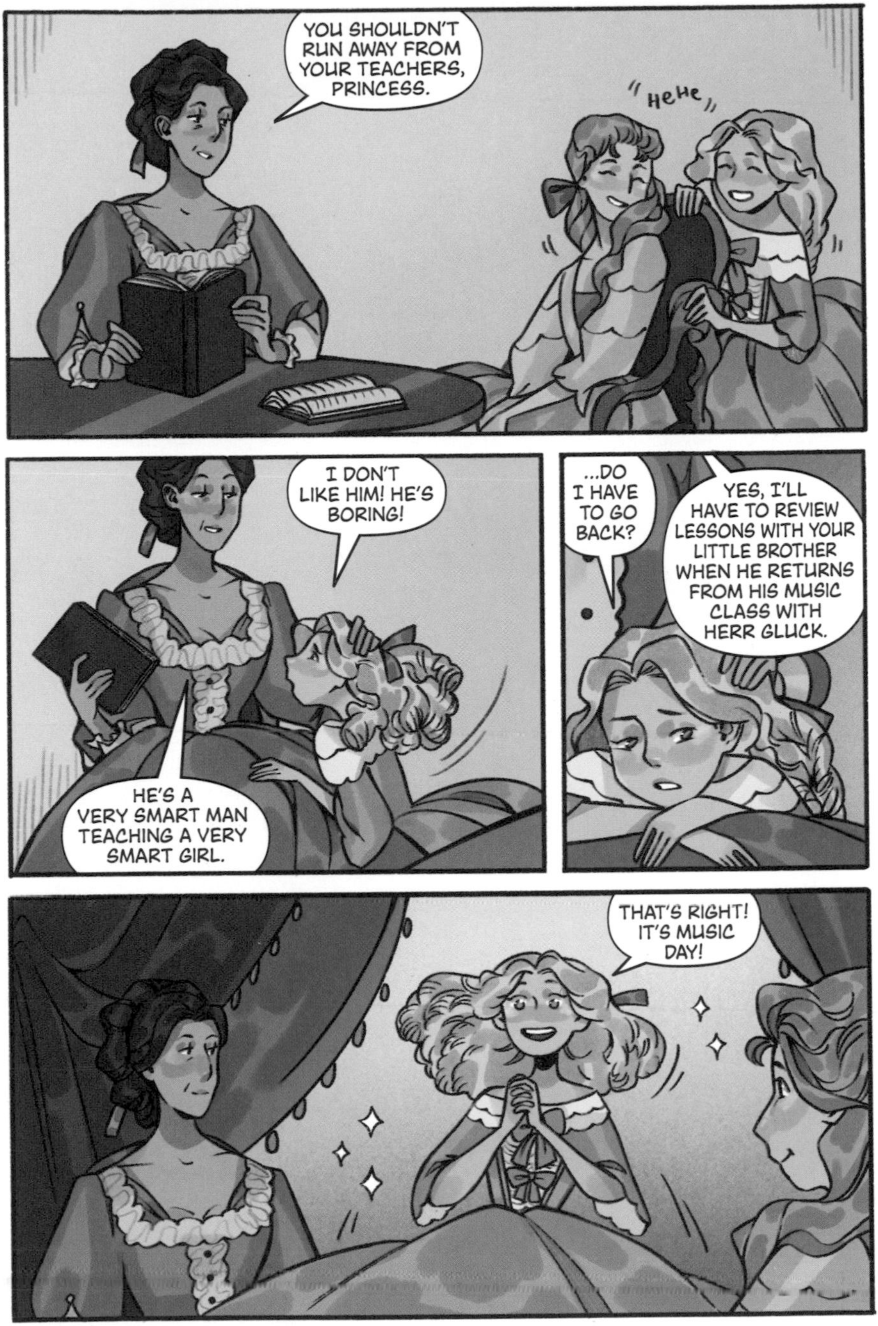
YOU SHOULDN'T RUN AWAY FROM YOUR TEACHERS, PRINCESS.
HEHE
I DON'T LIKE HIM! HE'S BORING!
HE'S A VERY SMART MAN TEACHING A VERY SMART GIRL.
...DO I HAVE TO GO BACK?
YES, I'LL HAVE TO REVIEW LESSONS WITH YOUR LITTLE BROTHER WHEN HE RETURNS FROM HIS MUSIC CLASS WITH HERR GLUCK.
THAT'S RIGHT! IT'S MUSIC DAY!

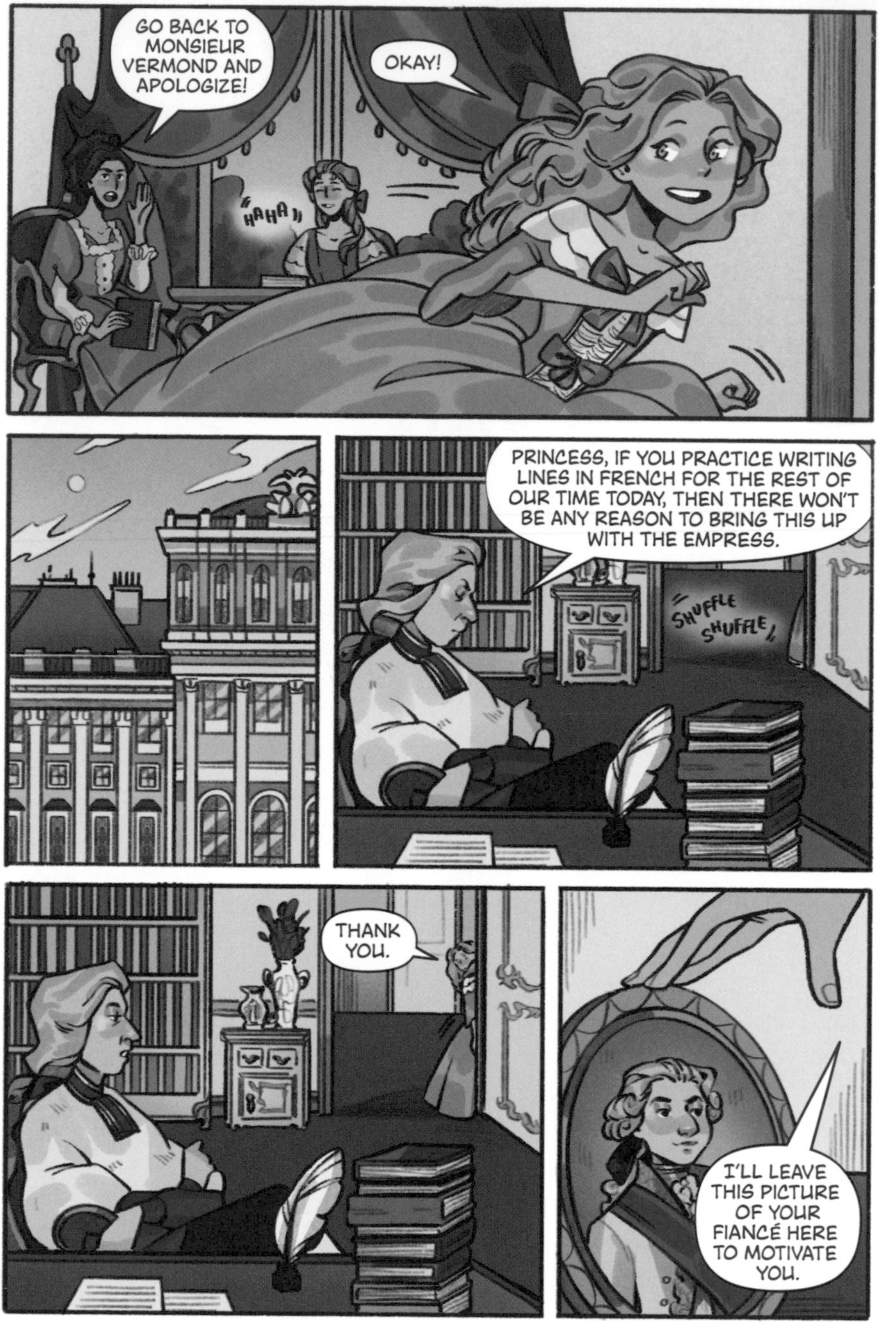
GO BACK TO MONSIEUR VERMOND AND APOLOGIZE!
OKAY!
"HAHA"
PRINCESS, IF YOU PRACTICE WRITING LINES IN FRENCH FOR THE REST OF OUR TIME TODAY, THEN THERE WON'T BE ANY REASON TO BRING THIS UP WITH THE EMPRESS.
"SHUFFLE SHUFFLE"
THANK YOU.
I'LL LEAVE THIS PICTURE OF YOUR FIANCÉ HERE TO MOTIVATE YOU.

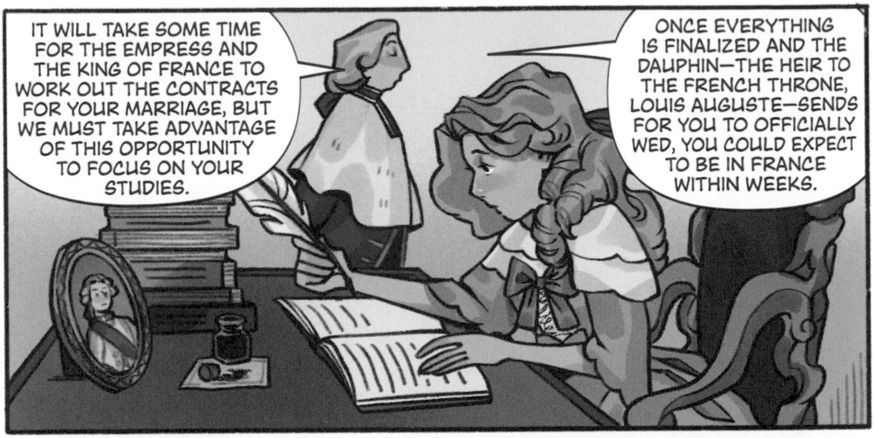
IT WILL TAKE SOME TIME FOR THE EMPRESS AND THE KING OF FRANCE TO WORK OUT THE CONTRACTS FOR YOUR MARRIAGE, BUT WE MUST TAKE ADVANTAGE OF THIS OPPORTUNITY TO FOCUS ON YOUR STUDIES.
ONCE EVERYTHING IS FINALIZED AND THE DAUPHIN—THE HEIR TO THE FRENCH THRONE, LOUIS AUGUSTE—SENDS FOR YOU TO OFFICIALLY WED, YOU COULD EXPECT TO BE IN FRANCE WITHIN WEEKS.

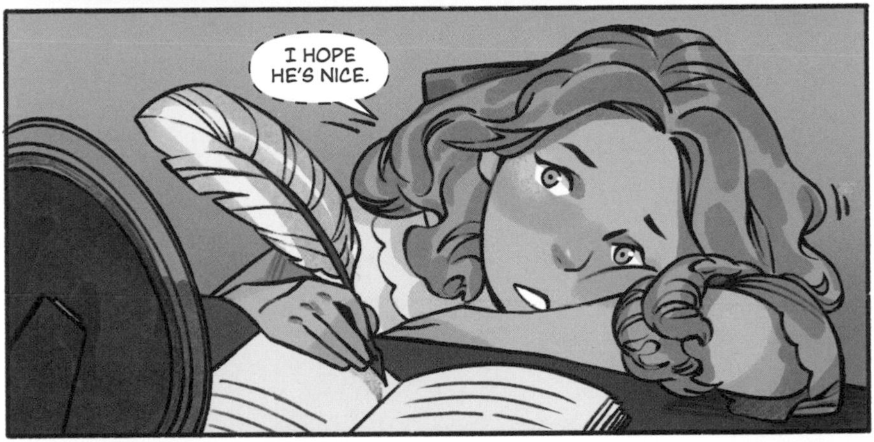
I HOPE HE'S NICE.

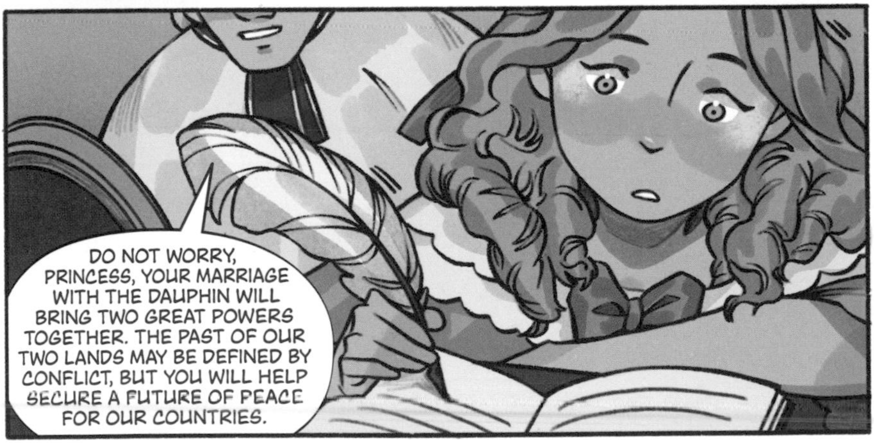
DO NOT WORRY, PRINCESS, YOUR MARRIAGE WITH THE DAUPHIN WILL BRING TWO GREAT POWERS TOGETHER. THE PAST OF OUR TWO LANDS MAY BE DEFINED BY CONFLICT, BUT YOU WILL HELP SECURE A FUTURE OF PEACE FOR OUR COUNTRIES.

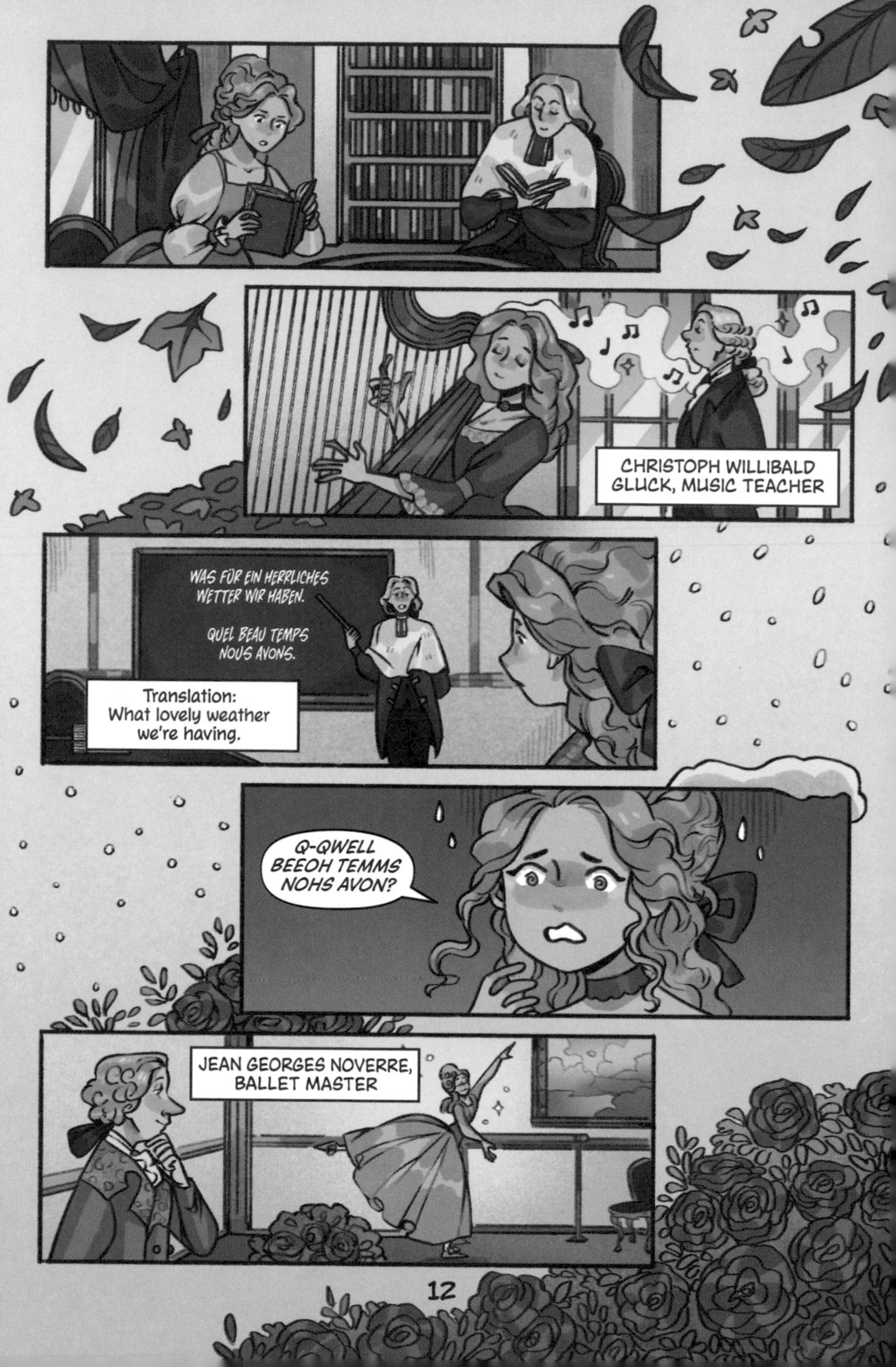
CHRISTOPH WILLIBALD GLUCK, MUSIC TEACHER
WAS FÜR EIN HERRLICHES WETTER WIR HABEN.
QUEL BEAU TEMPS NOUS AVONS.
Translation: What lovely weather we're having.
Q-QWELL BEEOH TEMMS NOHS AVON?
JEAN GEORGES NOVERRE, BALLET MASTER

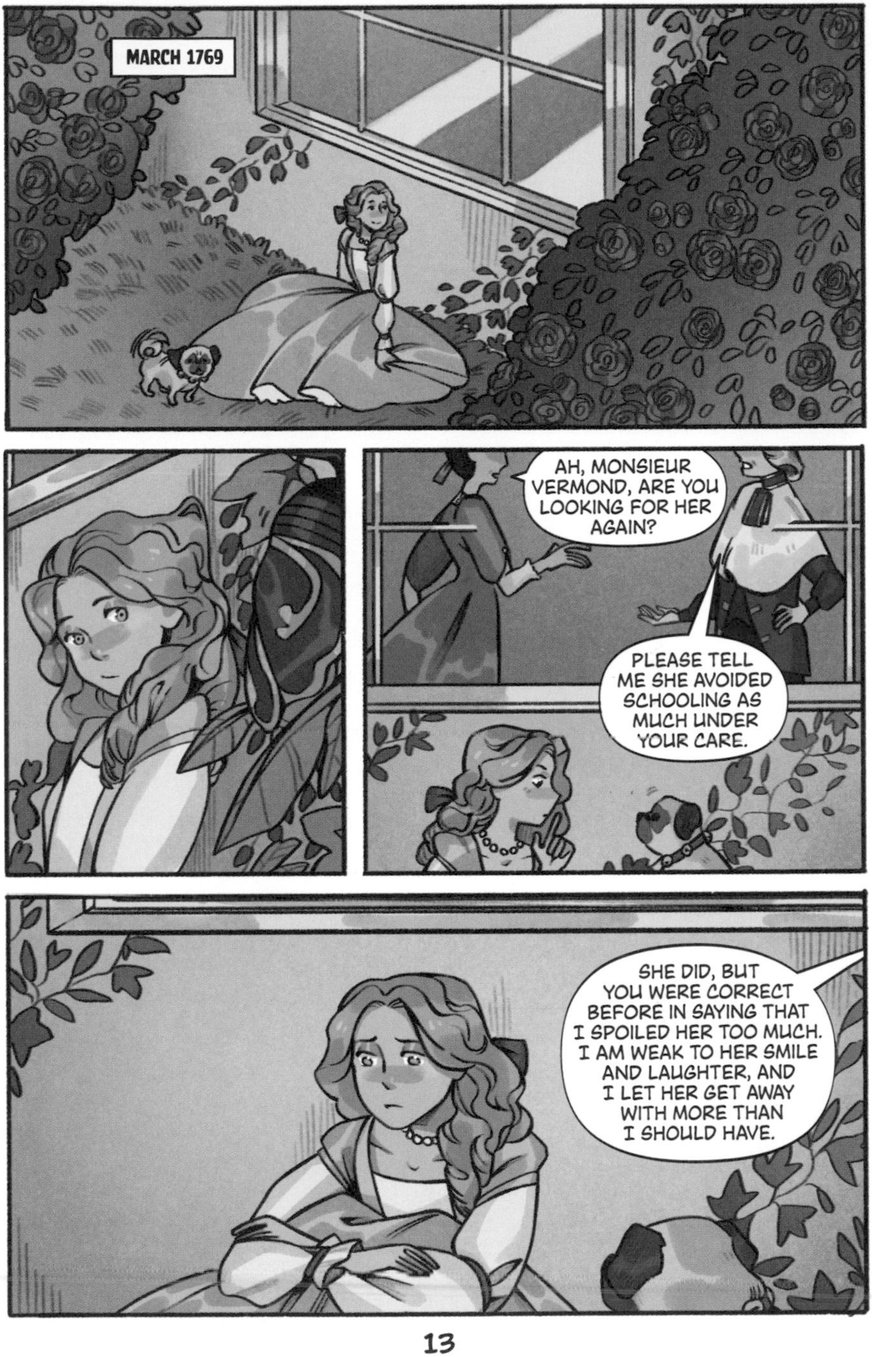
MARCH 1769
AH, MONSIEUR VERMOND, ARE YOU LOOKING FOR HER AGAIN?
PLEASE TELL ME SHE AVOIDED SCHOOLING AS MUCH UNDER YOUR CARE.
SHE DID, BUT YOU WERE CORRECT BEFORE IN SAYING THAT I SPOILED HER TOO MUCH. I AM WEAK TO HER SMILE AND LAUGHTER, AND I LET HER GET AWAY WITH MORE THAN I SHOULD HAVE.

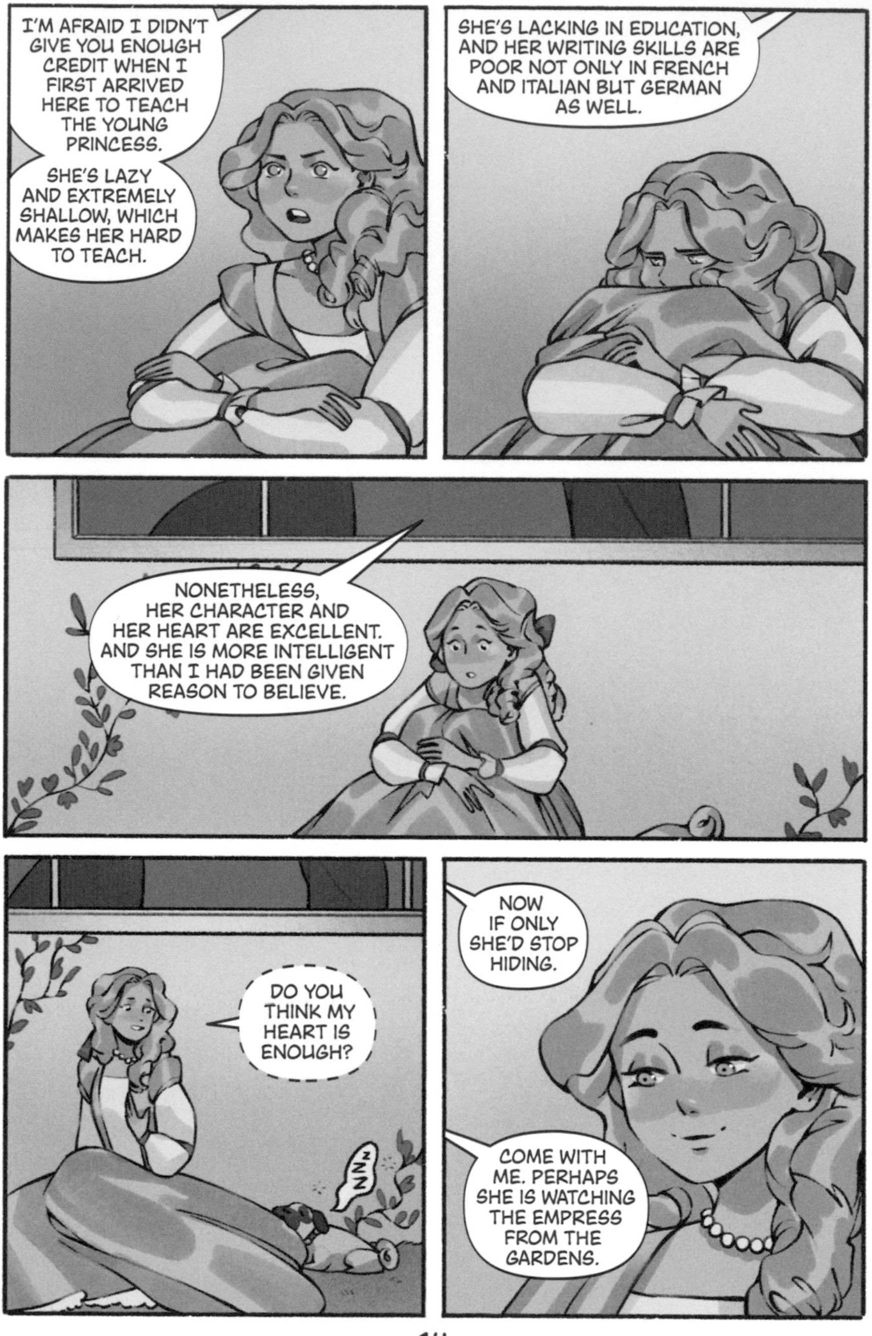
I'M AFRAID I DIDN'T GIVE YOU ENOUGH CREDIT WHEN I FIRST ARRIVED HERE TO TEACH THE YOUNG PRINCESS.
SHE'S LAZY AND EXTREMELY SHALLOW, WHICH MAKES HER HARD TO TEACH.
SHE'S LACKING IN EDUCATION, AND HER WRITING SKILLS ARE POOR NOT ONLY IN FRENCH AND ITALIAN BUT GERMAN AS WELL.
NONETHELESS, HER CHARACTER AND HER HEART ARE EXCELLENT. AND SHE IS MORE INTELLIGENT THAN I HAD BEEN GIVEN REASON TO BELIEVE.
DO YOU THINK MY HEART IS ENOUGH?
ZZZ
NOW IF ONLY SHE'D STOP HIDING.
COME WITH ME. PERHAPS SHE IS WATCHING THE EMPRESS FROM THE GARDENS.

Maria Theresa, Holy Roman Empress

Born on May 13, 1717, Maria Theresa was not originally the heir to the Holy Roman Empire, but she became the oldest surviving child of the royal Habsburg line. The Pragmatic Sanction of 1713 changed the law to allow her to inherit the empire as a woman and keep the Habsburgs in power—though the same power was not extended to her daughters.

Maria Theresa inherited the Holy Roman Empire in a weakened state, but she was able to build its strength and gain respect from not only her people but also the world. She promoted financial, medical, and educational reforms as well as commerce and agricultural development. No matter what, she was determined for her eldest son to inherit a stronger empire than she had.

One of her goals was to strengthen and grow the empire through the marriages of her children. And so she didn't take much of an interest in their early lives—she was largely absent from Maria Antonia's life until it came time to get her engaged to Louis Auguste.

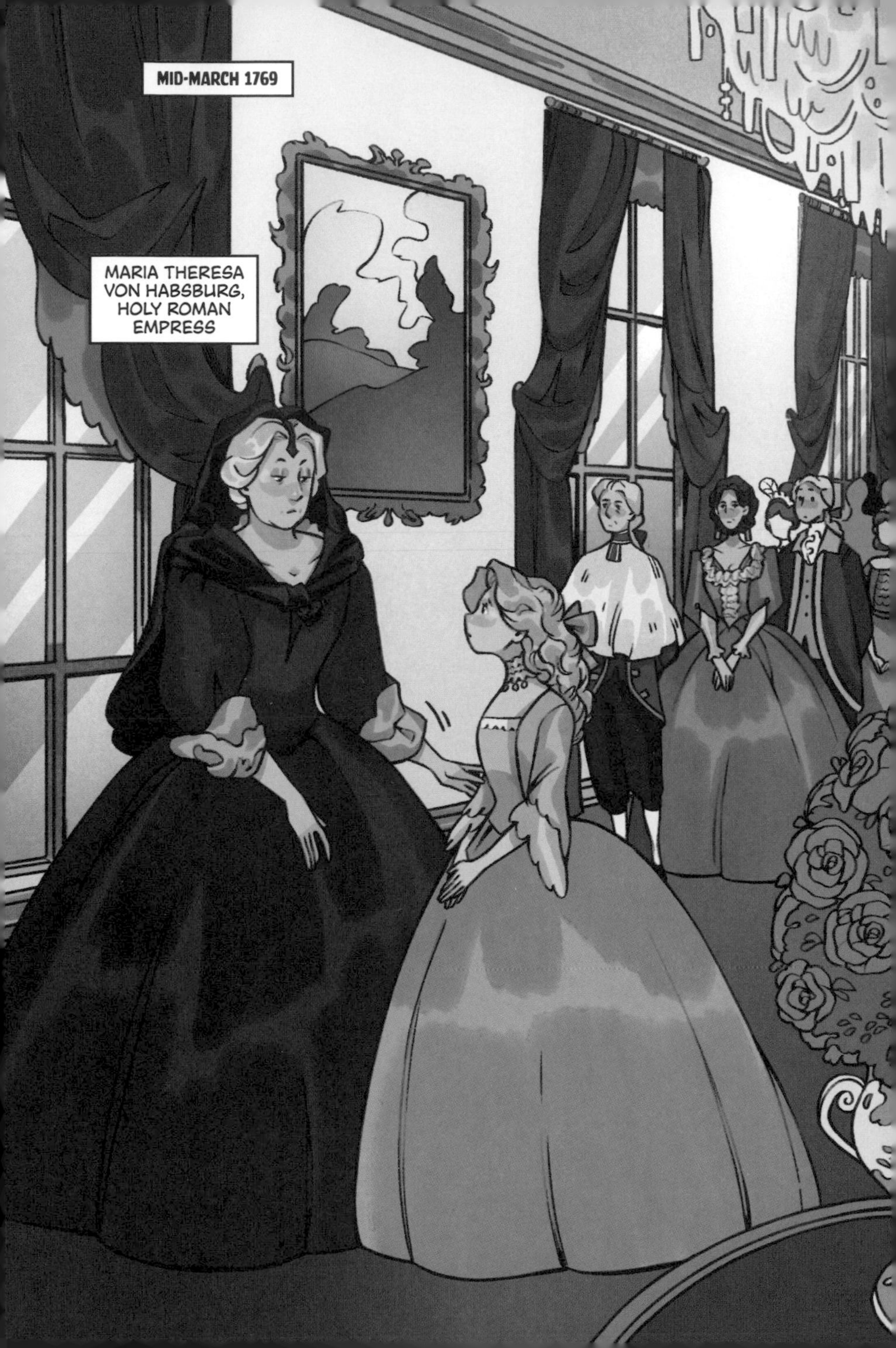
MID-MARCH 1769
MARIA THERESA VON HABSBURG, HOLY ROMAN EMPRESS

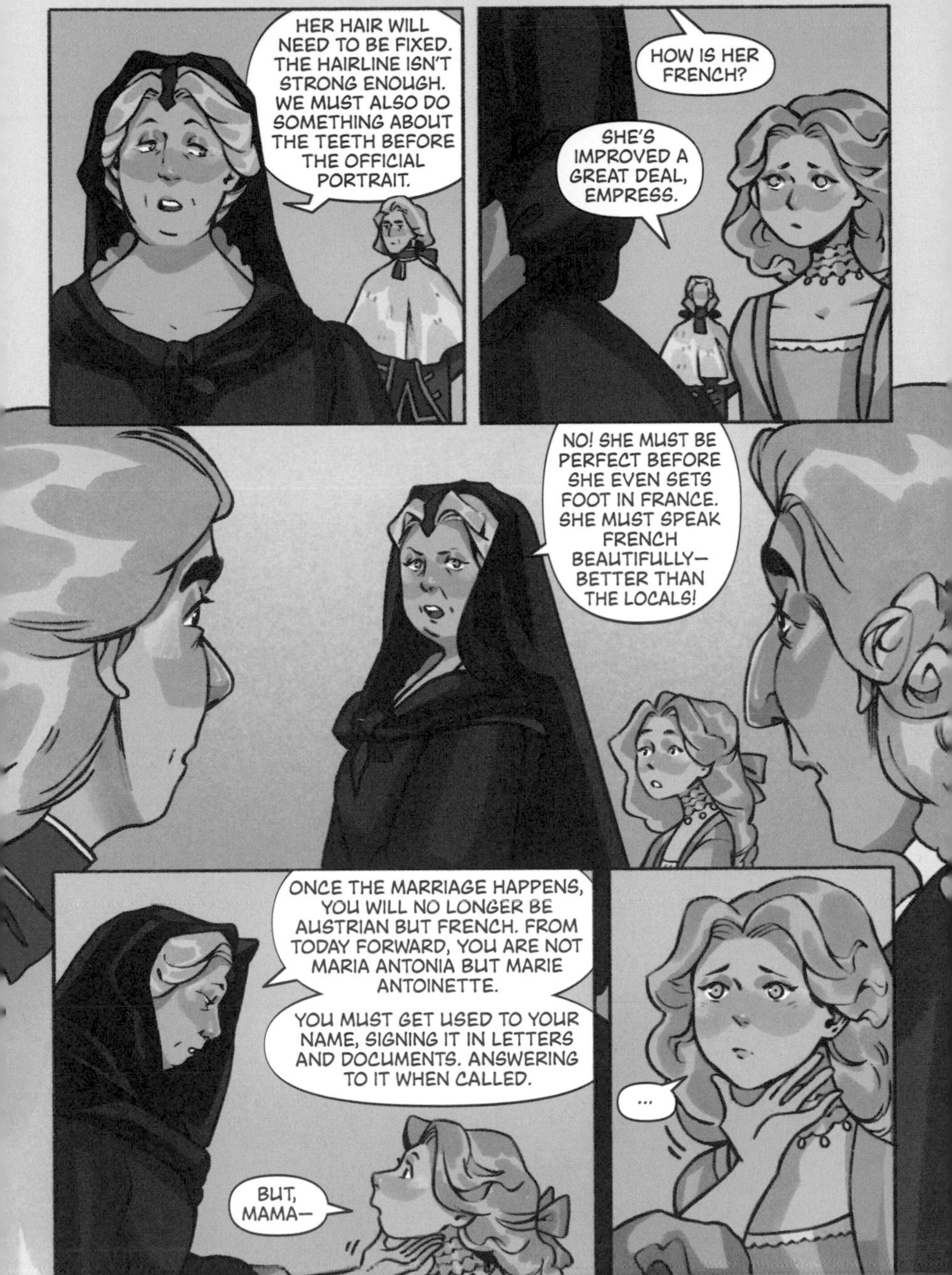
HER HAIR WILL NEED TO BE FIXED. THE HAIRLINE ISN'T STRONG ENOUGH. WE MUST ALSO DO SOMETHING ABOUT THE TEETH BEFORE THE OFFICIAL PORTRAIT.
HOW IS HER FRENCH?
SHE'S IMPROVED A GREAT DEAL, EMPRESS.
NO! SHE MUST BE PERFECT BEFORE SHE EVEN SETS FOOT IN FRANCE. SHE MUST SPEAK FRENCH BEAUTIFULLY—BETTER THAN THE LOCALS!
ONCE THE MARRIAGE HAPPENS, YOU WILL NO LONGER BE AUSTRIAN BUT FRENCH. FROM TODAY FORWARD, YOU ARE NOT MARIA ANTONIA BUT MARIE ANTOINETTE.
YOU MUST GET USED TO YOUR NAME, SIGNING IT IN LETTERS AND DOCUMENTS. ANSWERING TO IT WHEN CALLED.
BUT, MAMA—
...

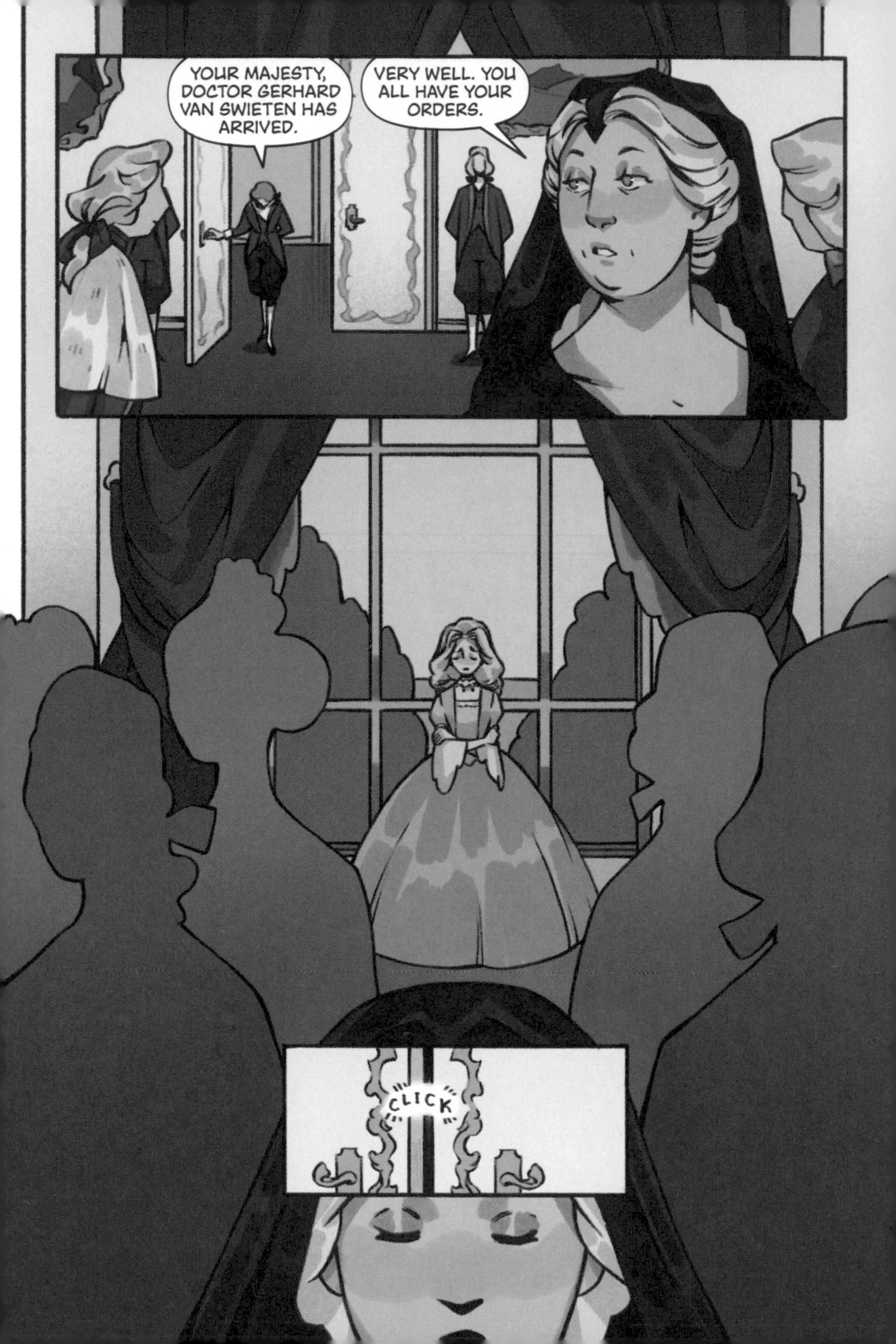
YOUR MAJESTY, DOCTOR GERHARD VAN SWIETEN HAS ARRIVED.
VERY WELL. YOU ALL HAVE YOUR ORDERS.
CLICK

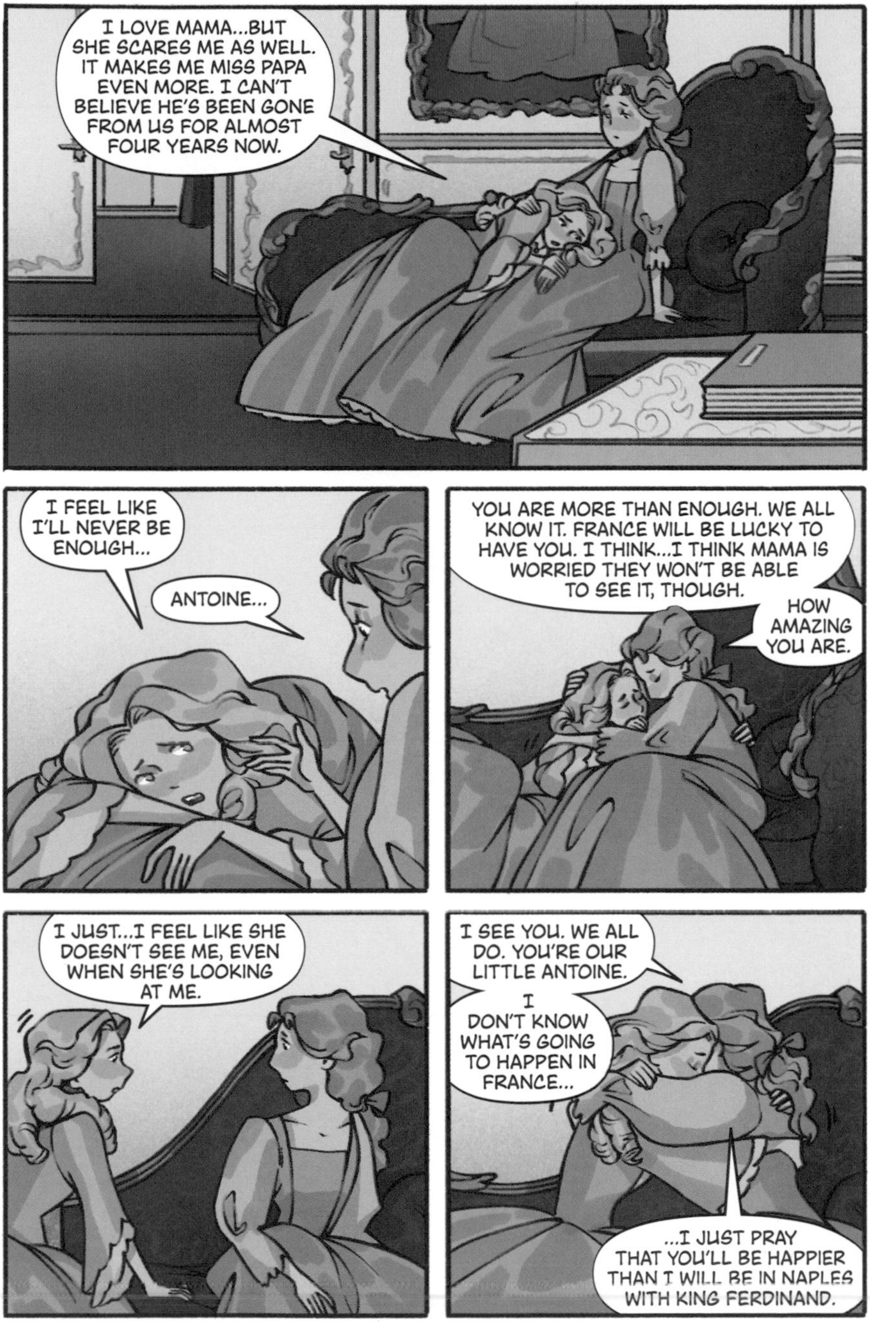

I LOVE MAMA...BUT SHE SCARES ME AS WELL. IT MAKES ME MISS PAPA EVEN MORE. I CAN'T BELIEVE HE'S BEEN GONE FROM US FOR ALMOST FOUR YEARS NOW.
I FEEL LIKE I'LL NEVER BE ENOUGH...
ANTOINE...
YOU ARE MORE THAN ENOUGH. WE ALL KNOW IT. FRANCE WILL BE LUCKY TO HAVE YOU. I THINK...I THINK MAMA IS WORRIED THEY WON'T BE ABLE TO SEE IT, THOUGH.
HOW AMAZING YOU ARE.
I JUST...I FEEL LIKE SHE DOESN'T SEE ME, EVEN WHEN SHE'S LOOKING AT ME.
I SEE YOU. WE ALL DO. YOU'RE OUR LITTLE ANTOINE.
I DON'T KNOW WHAT'S GOING TO HAPPEN IN FRANCE...
...I JUST PRAY THAT YOU'LL BE HAPPIER THAN I WILL BE IN NAPLES WITH KING FERDINAND.

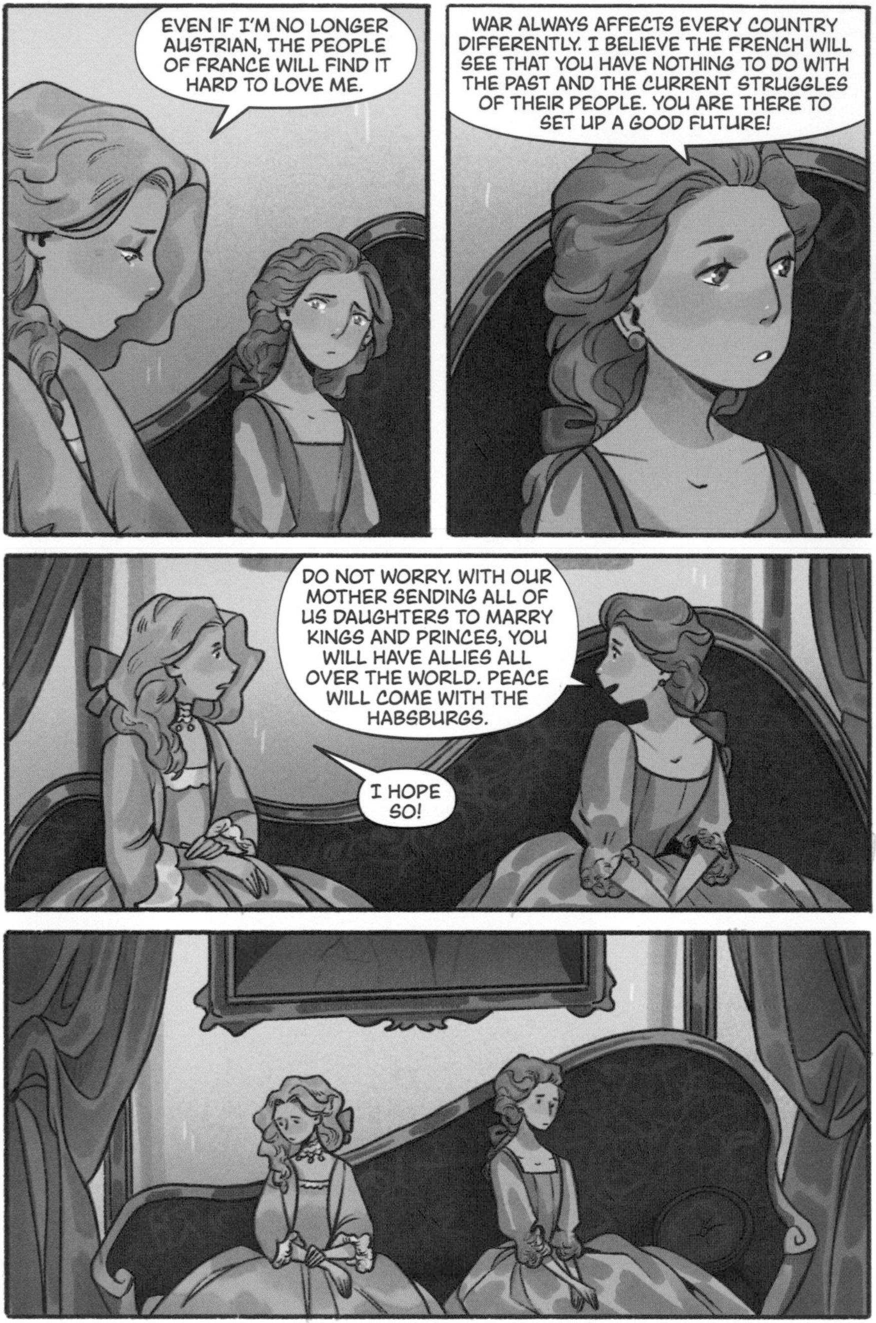
EVEN IF I'M NO LONGER AUSTRIAN, THE PEOPLE OF FRANCE WILL FIND IT HARD TO LOVE ME.
WAR ALWAYS AFFECTS EVERY COUNTRY DIFFERENTLY. I BELIEVE THE FRENCH WILL SEE THAT YOU HAVE NOTHING TO DO WITH THE PAST AND THE CURRENT STRUGGLES OF THEIR PEOPLE. YOU ARE THERE TO SET UP A GOOD FUTURE!
DO NOT WORRY. WITH OUR MOTHER SENDING ALL OF US DAUGHTERS TO MARRY KINGS AND PRINCES, YOU WILL HAVE ALLIES ALL OVER THE WORLD. PEACE WILL COME WITH THE HABSBURGS.
I HOPE SO!

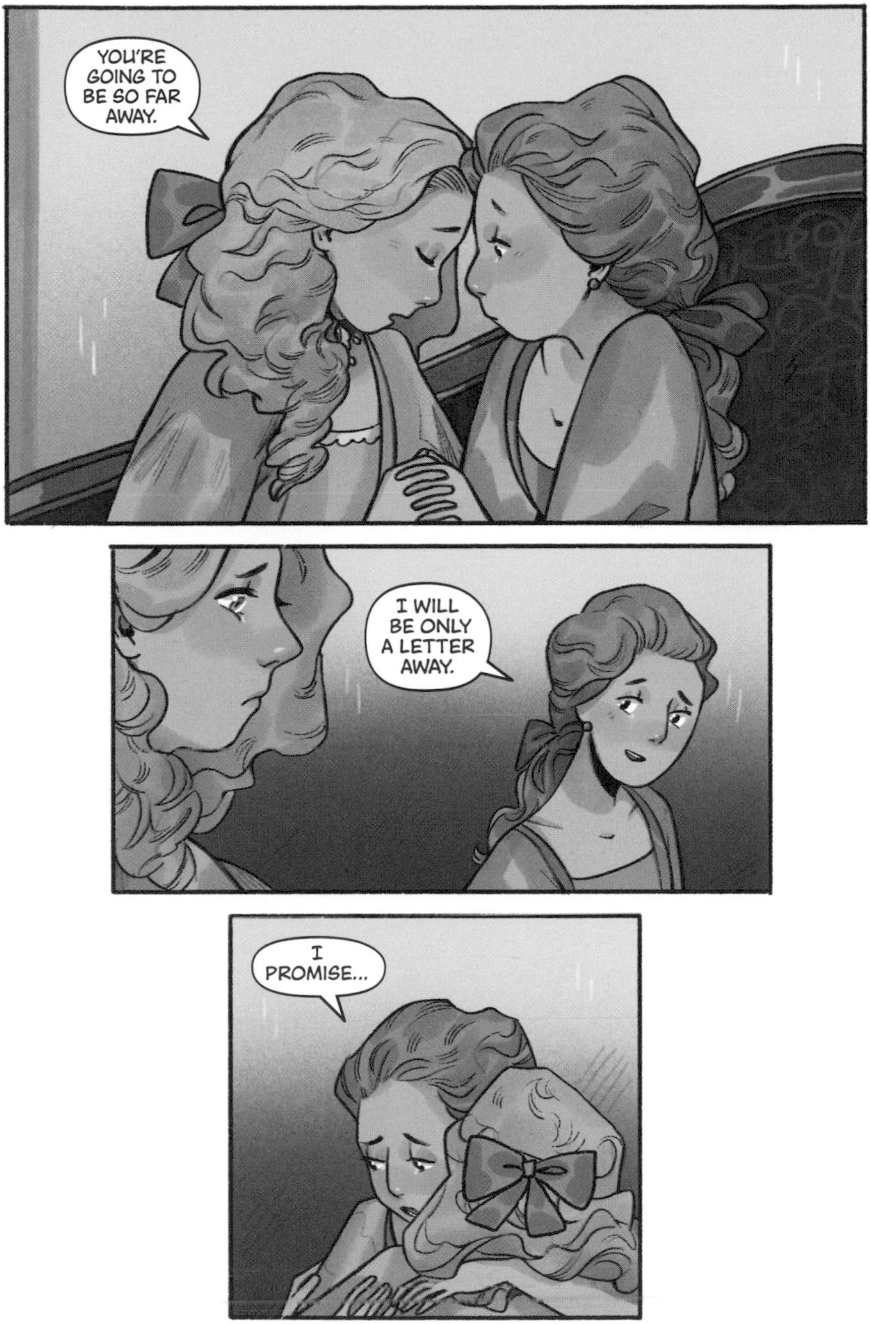
YOU'RE GOING TO BE SO FAR AWAY.
I WILL BE ONLY A LETTER AWAY.
I PROMISE...

The Seven Years' War

The Seven Years' War is considered the first true world war, involving five of the seven continents: Europe, North America, South America, Africa, and Asia. A major cause was Great Britain and France's struggle for control over North America. The war lasted from May 17, 1756, to February 15, 1763—just a few months short of seven full years. Austria had used the war to try to gain land it had lost in an earlier war, causing many countries, including France, to blame it for their losses.

Over half a million people died in the Seven Years' War, and the cost of it affected many countries' economies, causing a greater divide between the wealth of the upper and lower classes. This was especially felt in France, which lost all of its land in North America and a lot of its income.

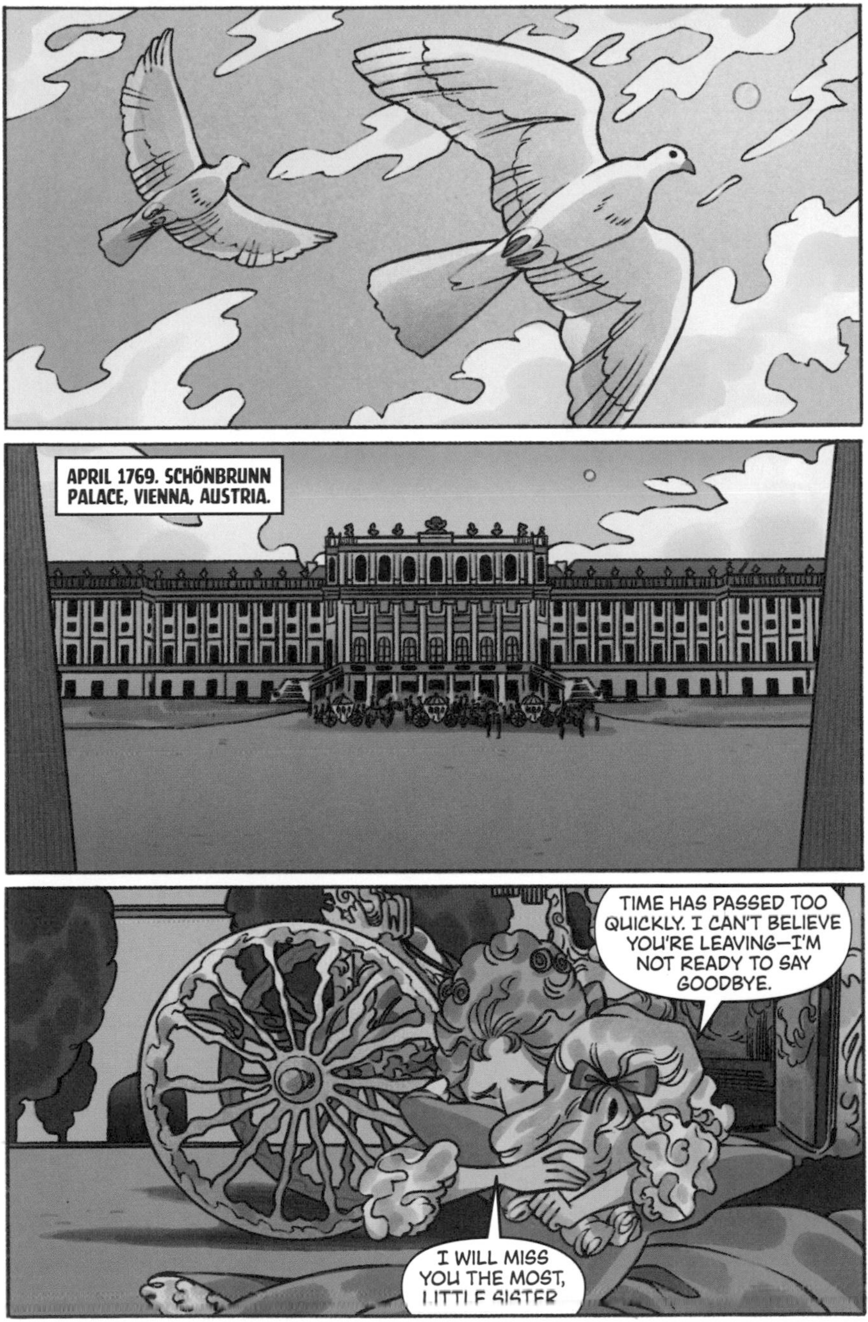
APRIL 1769. SCHÖNBRUNN PALACE, VIENNA, AUSTRIA.
TIME HAS PASSED TOO QUICKLY. I CAN'T BELIEVE YOU'RE LEAVING—I'M NOT READY TO SAY GOODBYE.
I WILL MISS YOU THE MOST, LITTLE SISTER

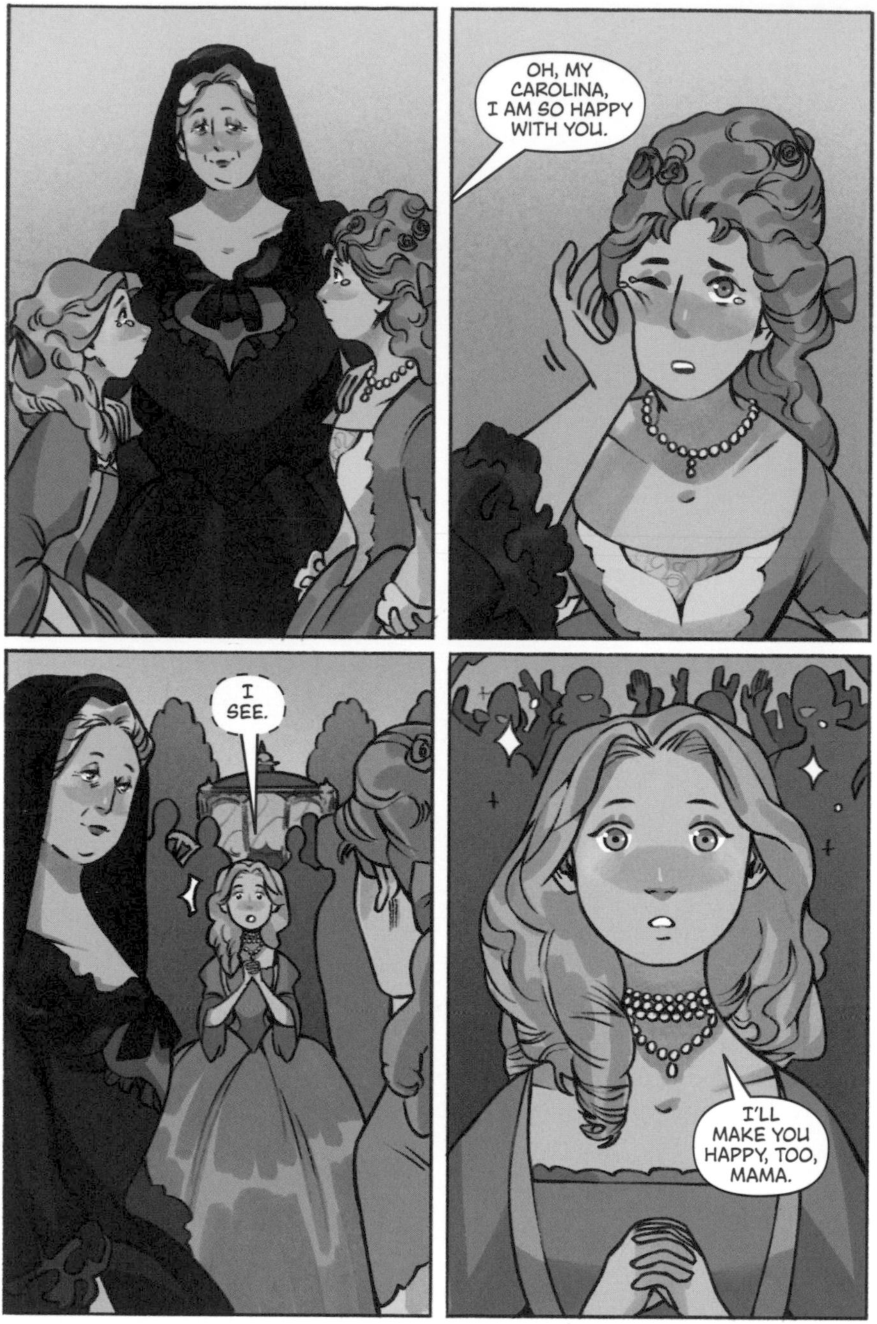
OH, MY CAROLINA, I AM SO HAPPY WITH YOU.
I SEE.
I'LL MAKE YOU HAPPY, TOO, MAMA.

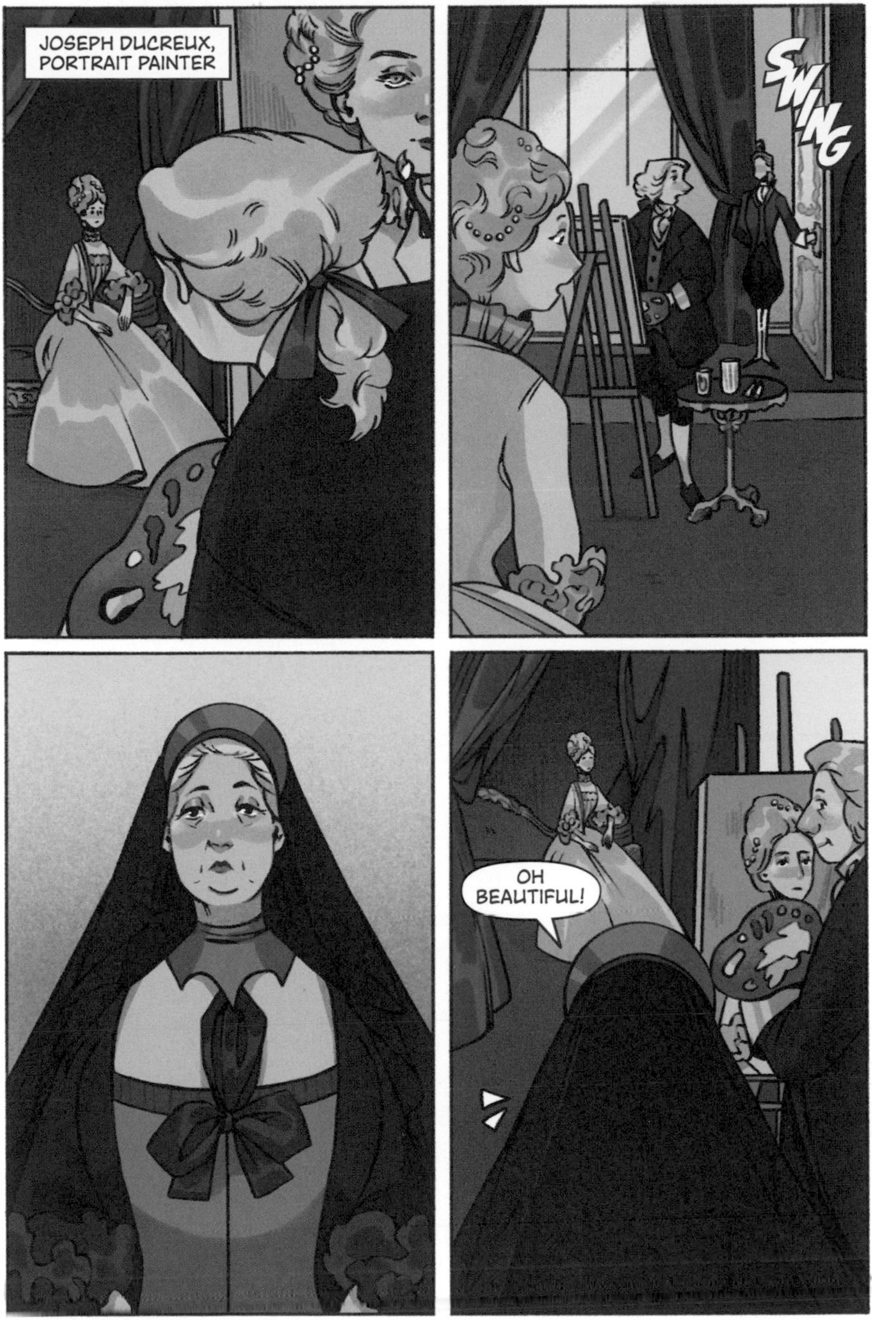
JOSEPH DUCREUX, PORTRAIT PAINTER
SWING
OH BEAUTIFUL!

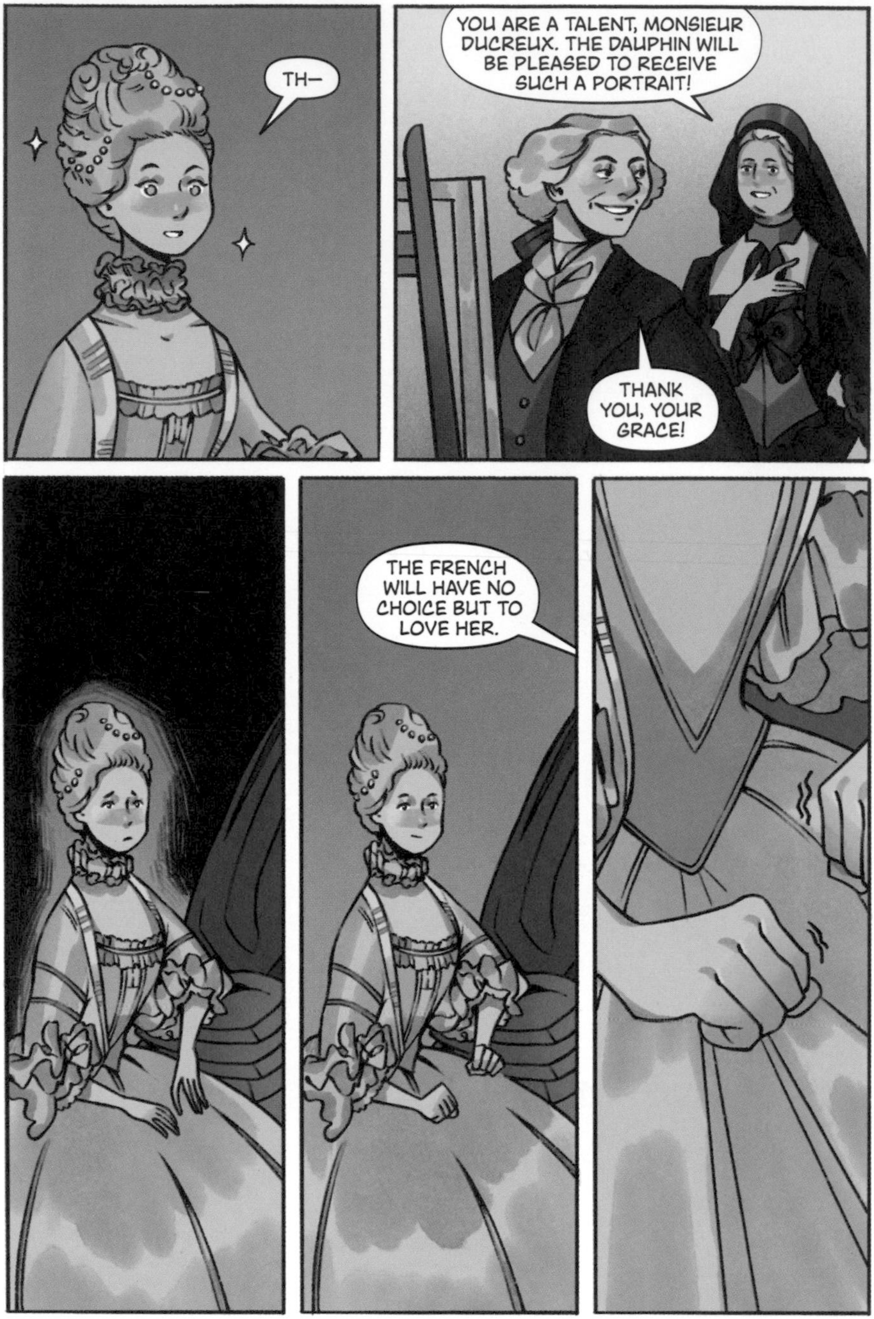
TH–
YOU ARE A TALENT, MONSIEUR DUCREUX. THE DAUPHIN WILL BE PLEASED TO RECEIVE SUCH A PORTRAIT!
THANK YOU, YOUR GRACE!
THE FRENCH WILL HAVE NO CHOICE BUT TO LOVE HER.

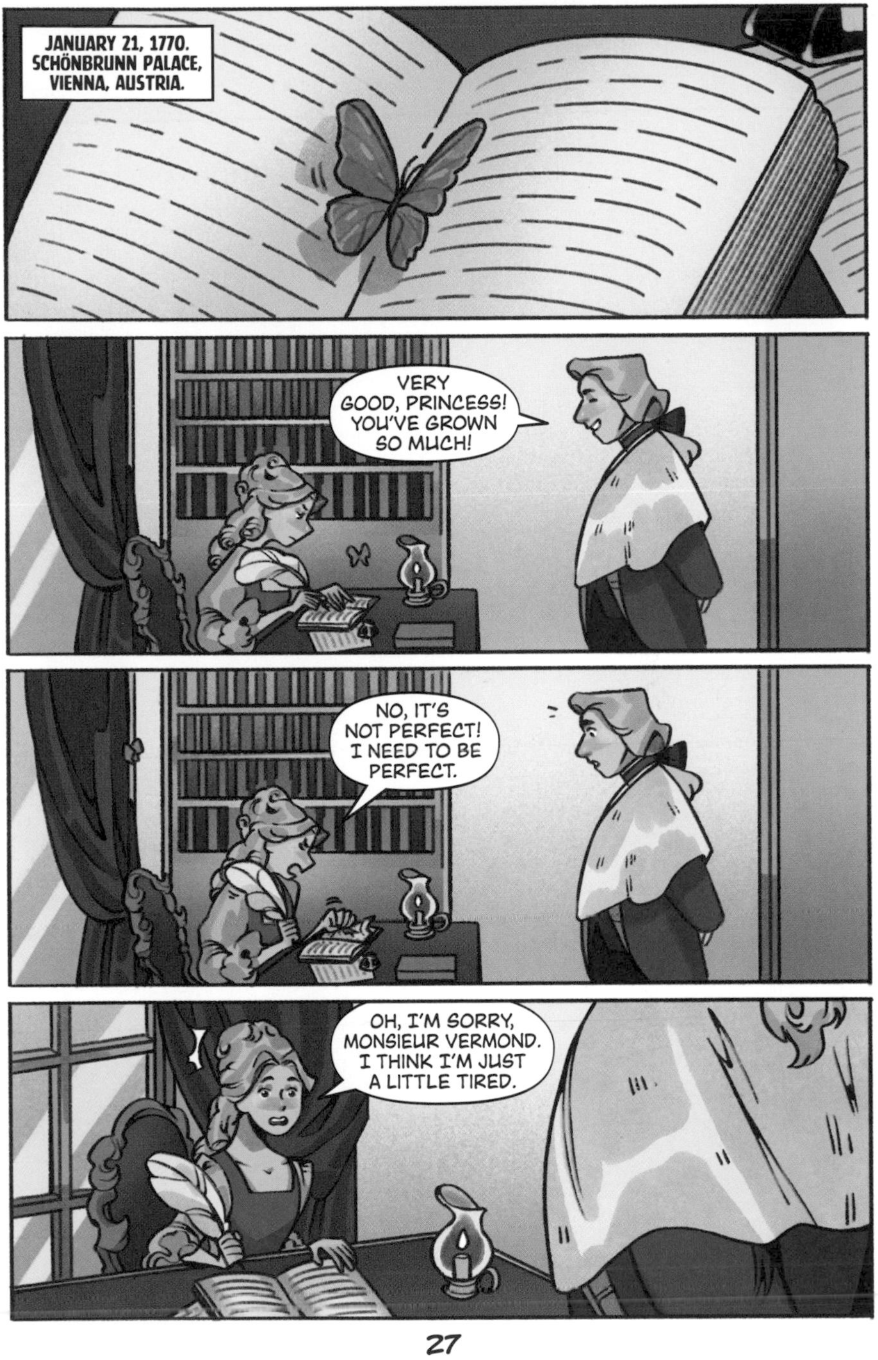
JANUARY 21, 1770. SCHÖNBRUNN PALACE, VIENNA, AUSTRIA.
VERY GOOD, PRINCESS! YOU'VE GROWN SO MUCH!
NO, IT'S NOT PERFECT! I NEED TO BE PERFECT.
OH, I'M SORRY, MONSIEUR VERMOND. I THINK I'M JUST A LITTLE TIRED.

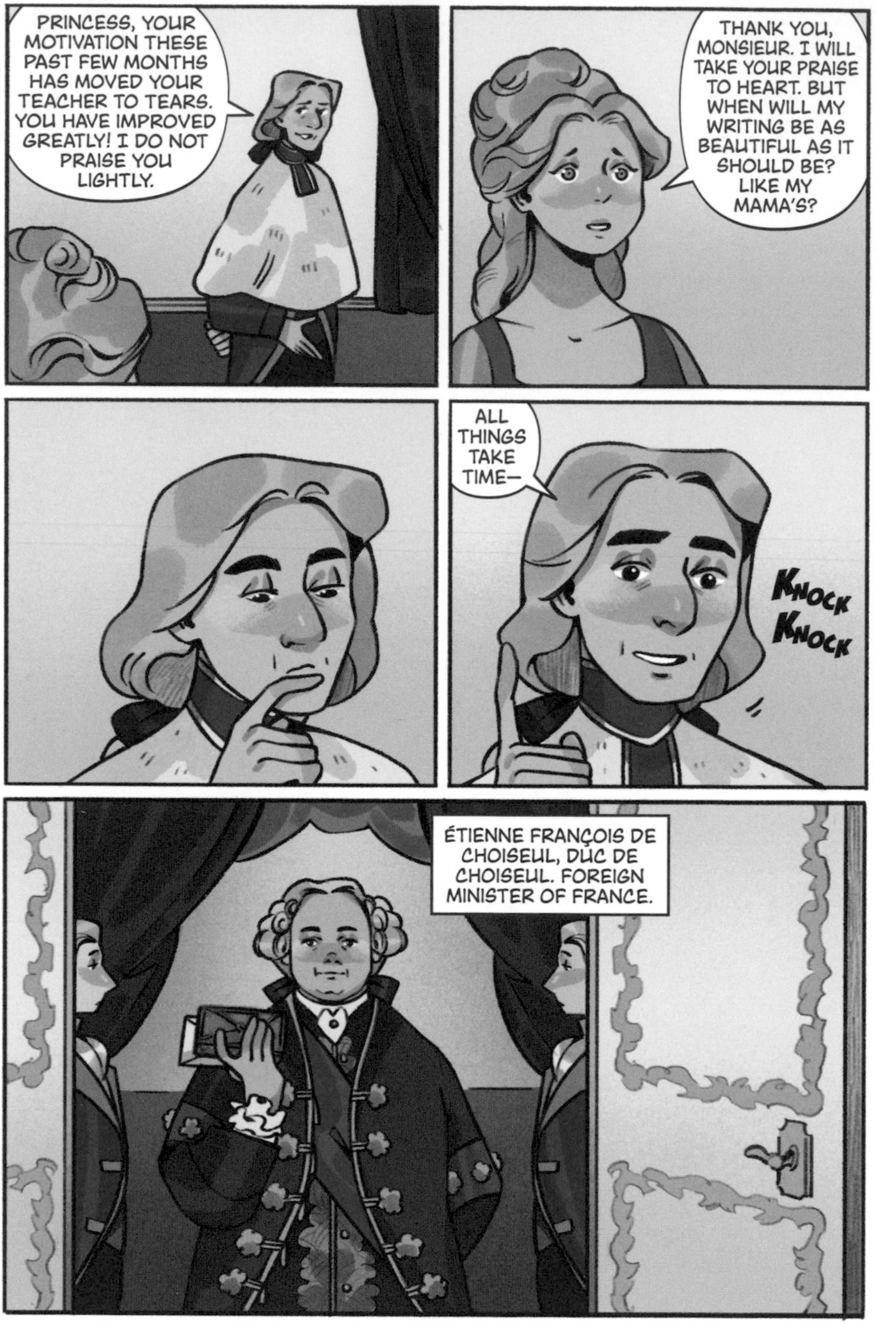
PRINCESS, YOUR MOTIVATION THESE PAST FEW MONTHS HAS MOVED YOUR TEACHER TO TEARS. YOU HAVE IMPROVED GREATLY! I DO NOT PRAISE YOU LIGHTLY.
THANK YOU, MONSIEUR. I WILL TAKE YOUR PRAISE TO HEART. BUT WHEN WILL MY WRITING BE AS BEAUTIFUL AS IT SHOULD BE? LIKE MY MAMA'S?
ALL THINGS TAKE TIME—
KNOCK KNOCK
ÉTIENNE FRANÇOIS DE CHOISEUL, DUC DE CHOISEUL. FOREIGN MINISTER OF FRANCE.

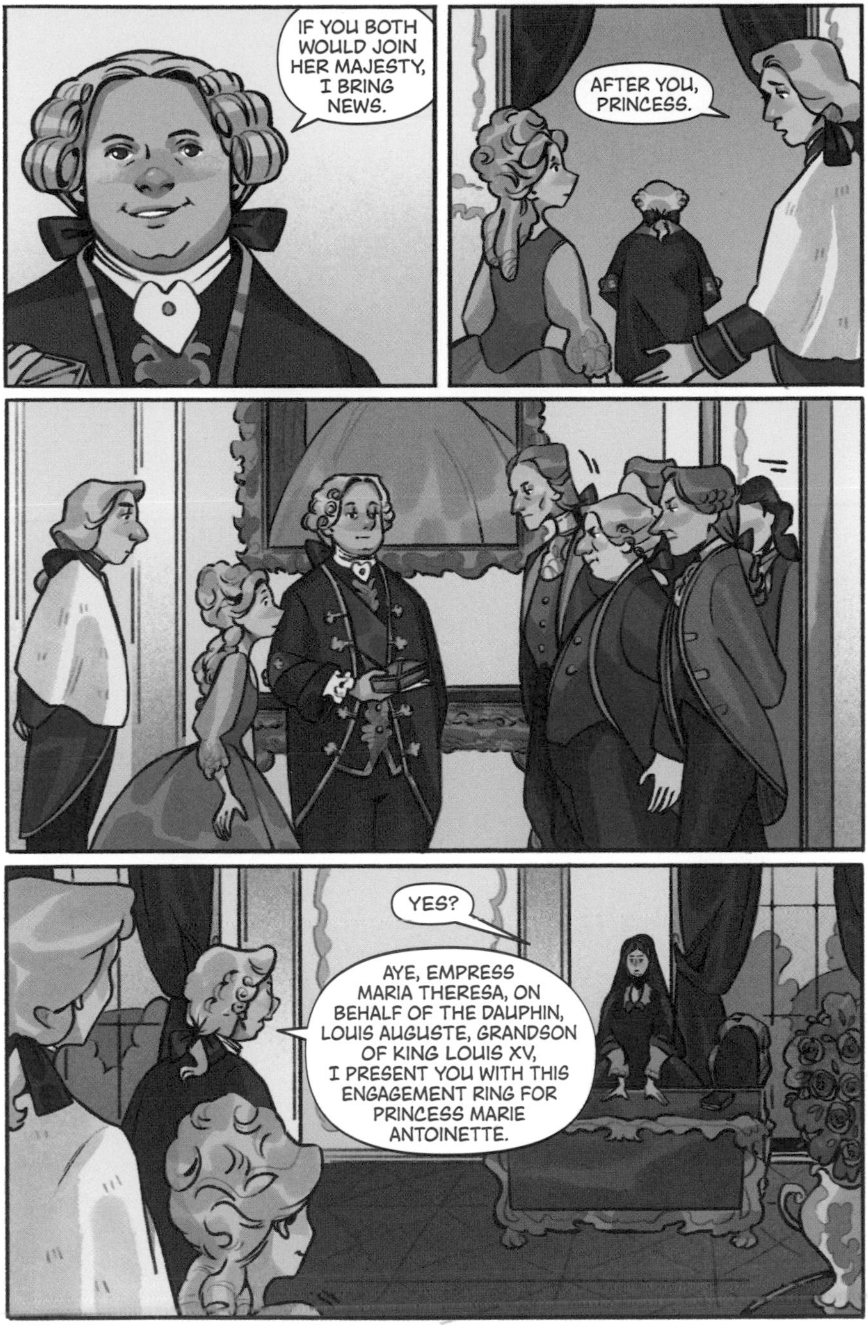
IF YOU BOTH WOULD JOIN HER MAJESTY, I BRING NEWS.
AFTER YOU, PRINCESS.
YES?
AYE, EMPRESS MARIA THERESA, ON BEHALF OF THE DAUPHIN, LOUIS AUGUSTE, GRANDSON OF KING LOUIS XV, I PRESENT YOU WITH THIS ENGAGEMENT RING FOR PRINCESS MARIE ANTOINETTE.

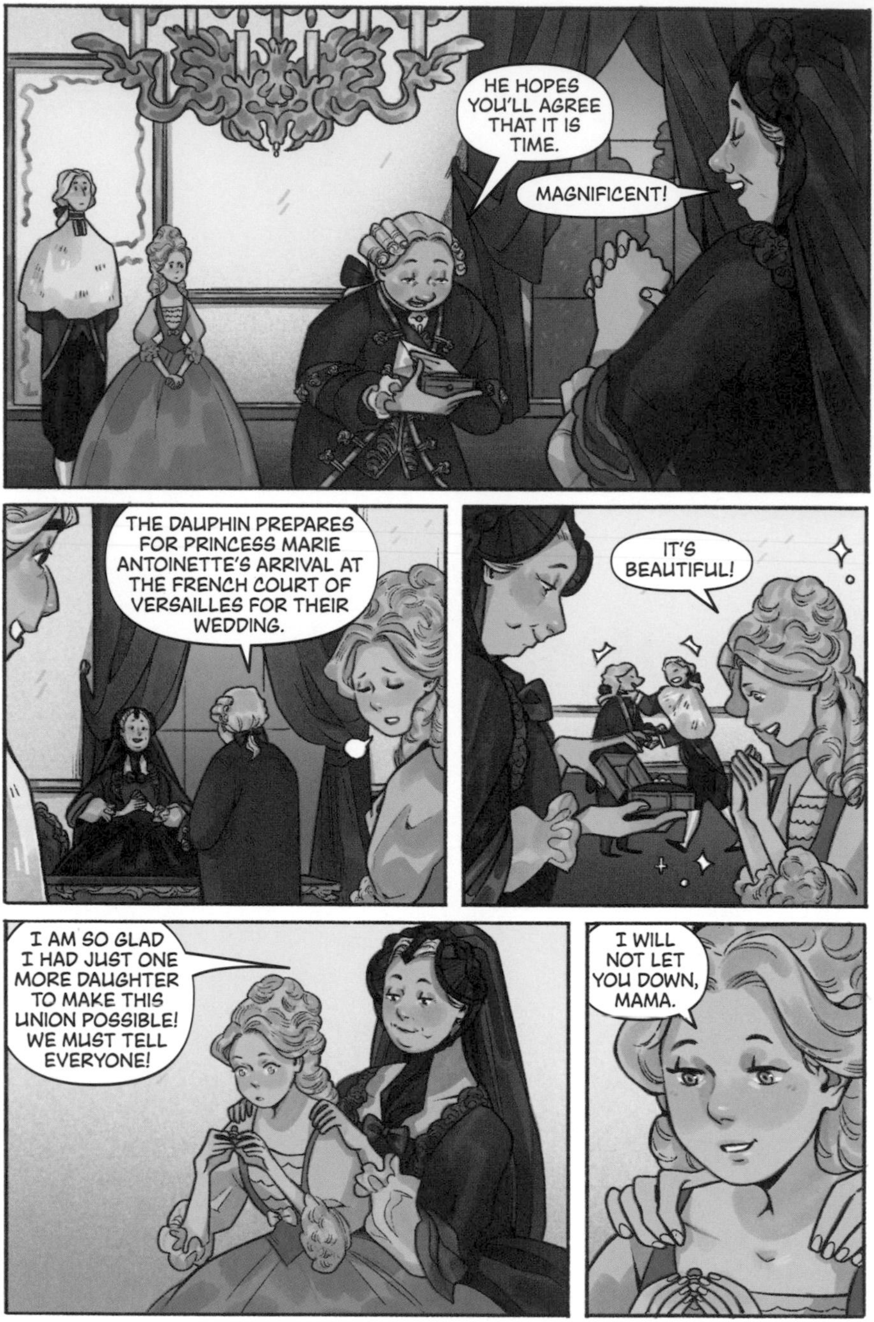
HE HOPES YOU'LL AGREE THAT IT IS TIME.
MAGNIFICENT!
THE DAUPHIN PREPARES FOR PRINCESS MARIE ANTOINETTE'S ARRIVAL AT THE FRENCH COURT OF VERSAILLES FOR THEIR WEDDING.
IT'S BEAUTIFUL!
I AM SO GLAD I HAD JUST ONE MORE DAUGHTER TO MAKE THIS UNION POSSIBLE! WE MUST TELL EVERYONE!
I WILL NOT LET YOU DOWN, MAMA.

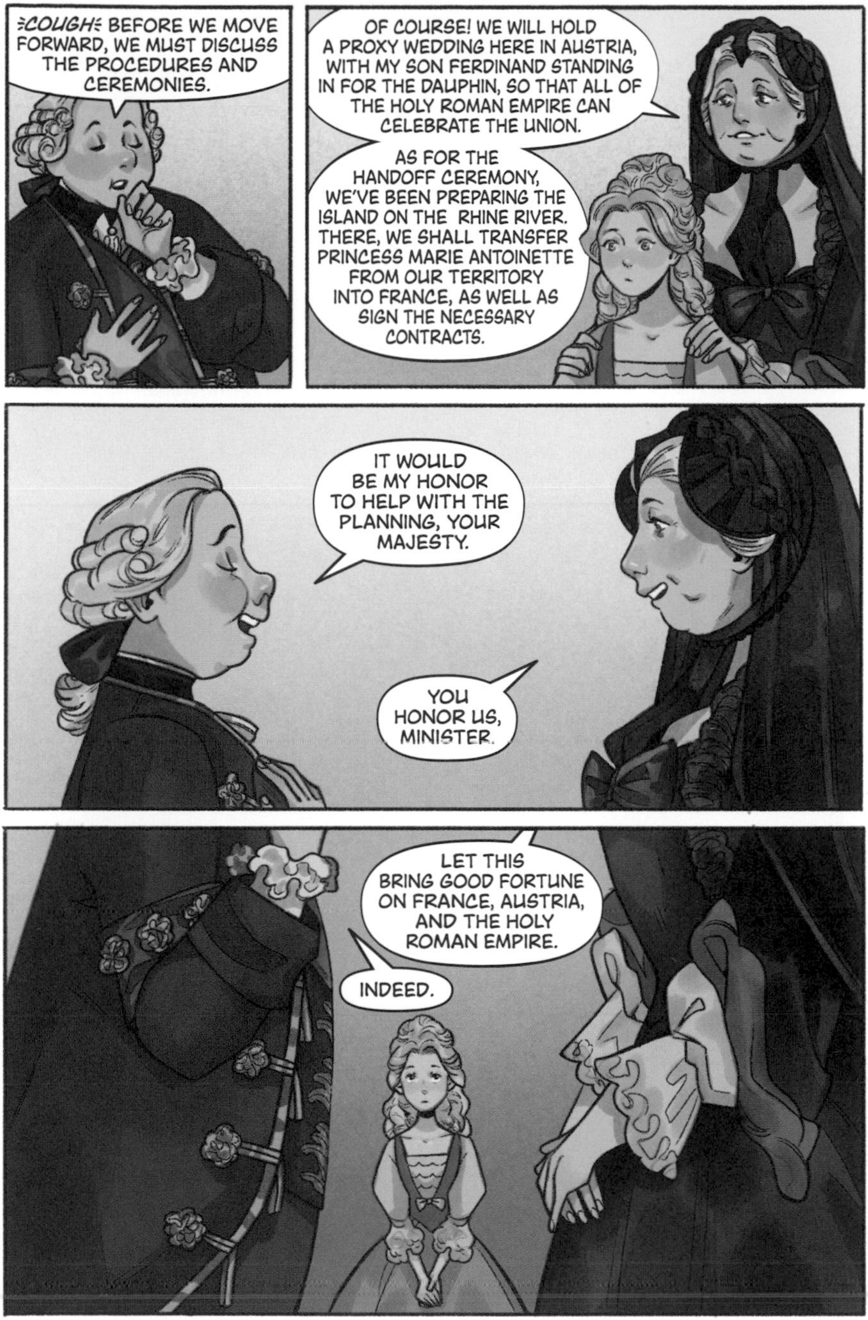

=COUGH= BEFORE WE MOVE FORWARD, WE MUST DISCUSS THE PROCEDURES AND CEREMONIES.
OF COURSE! WE WILL HOLD A PROXY WEDDING HERE IN AUSTRIA, WITH MY SON FERDINAND STANDING IN FOR THE DAUPHIN, SO THAT ALL OF THE HOLY ROMAN EMPIRE CAN CELEBRATE THE UNION.
AS FOR THE HANDOFF CEREMONY, WE'VE BEEN PREPARING THE ISLAND ON THE RHINE RIVER. THERE, WE SHALL TRANSFER PRINCESS MARIE ANTOINETTE FROM OUR TERRITORY INTO FRANCE, AS WELL AS SIGN THE NECESSARY CONTRACTS.
IT WOULD BE MY HONOR TO HELP WITH THE PLANNING, YOUR MAJESTY.
YOU HONOR US, MINISTER.
LET THIS BRING GOOD FORTUNE ON FRANCE, AUSTRIA, AND THE HOLY ROMAN EMPIRE.
INDEED.

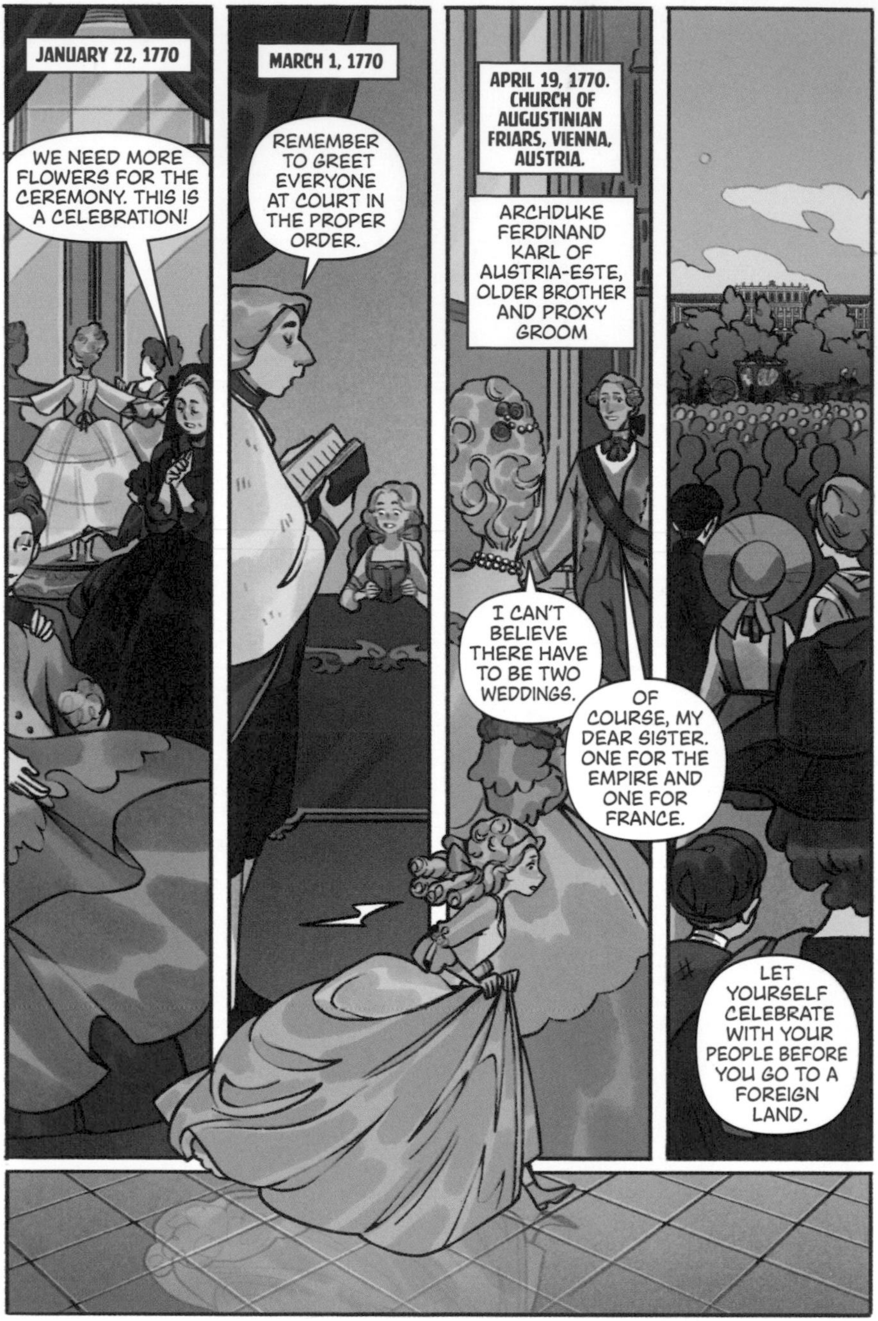
JANUARY 22, 1770
WE NEED MORE FLOWERS FOR THE CEREMONY. THIS IS A CELEBRATION!
MARCH 1, 1770
REMEMBER TO GREET EVERYONE AT COURT IN THE PROPER ORDER.
APRIL 19, 1770. CHURCH OF AUGUSTINIAN FRIARS, VIENNA, AUSTRIA.
ARCHDUKE FERDINAND KARL OF AUSTRIA-ESTE, OLDER BROTHER AND PROXY GROOM
I CAN'T BELIEVE THERE HAVE TO BE TWO WEDDINGS.
OF COURSE, MY DEAR SISTER. ONE FOR THE EMPIRE AND ONE FOR FRANCE.
LET YOURSELF CELEBRATE WITH YOUR PEOPLE BEFORE YOU GO TO A FOREIGN LAND.

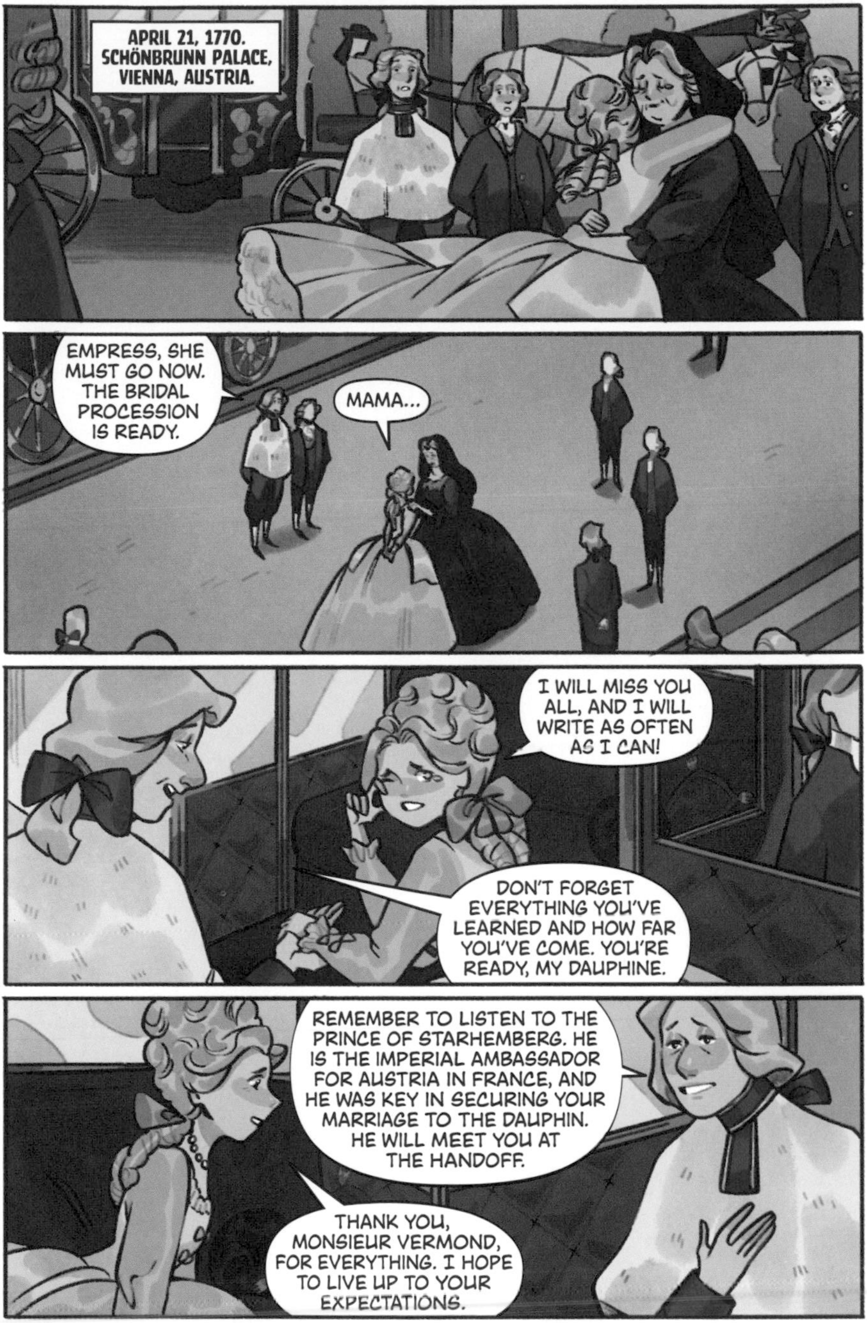
APRIL 21, 1770. SCHÖNBRUNN PALACE, VIENNA, AUSTRIA.
EMPRESS, SHE MUST GO NOW. THE BRIDAL PROCESSION IS READY.
MAMA...
I WILL MISS YOU ALL, AND I WILL WRITE AS OFTEN AS I CAN!
DON'T FORGET EVERYTHING YOU'VE LEARNED AND HOW FAR YOU'VE COME. YOU'RE READY, MY DAUPHINE.
REMEMBER TO LISTEN TO THE PRINCE OF STARHEMBERG. HE IS THE IMPERIAL AMBASSADOR FOR AUSTRIA IN FRANCE, AND HE WAS KEY IN SECURING YOUR MARRIAGE TO THE DAUPHIN. HE WILL MEET YOU AT THE HANDOFF.
THANK YOU, MONSIEUR VERMOND, FOR EVERYTHING. I HOPE TO LIVE UP TO YOUR EXPECTATIONS.

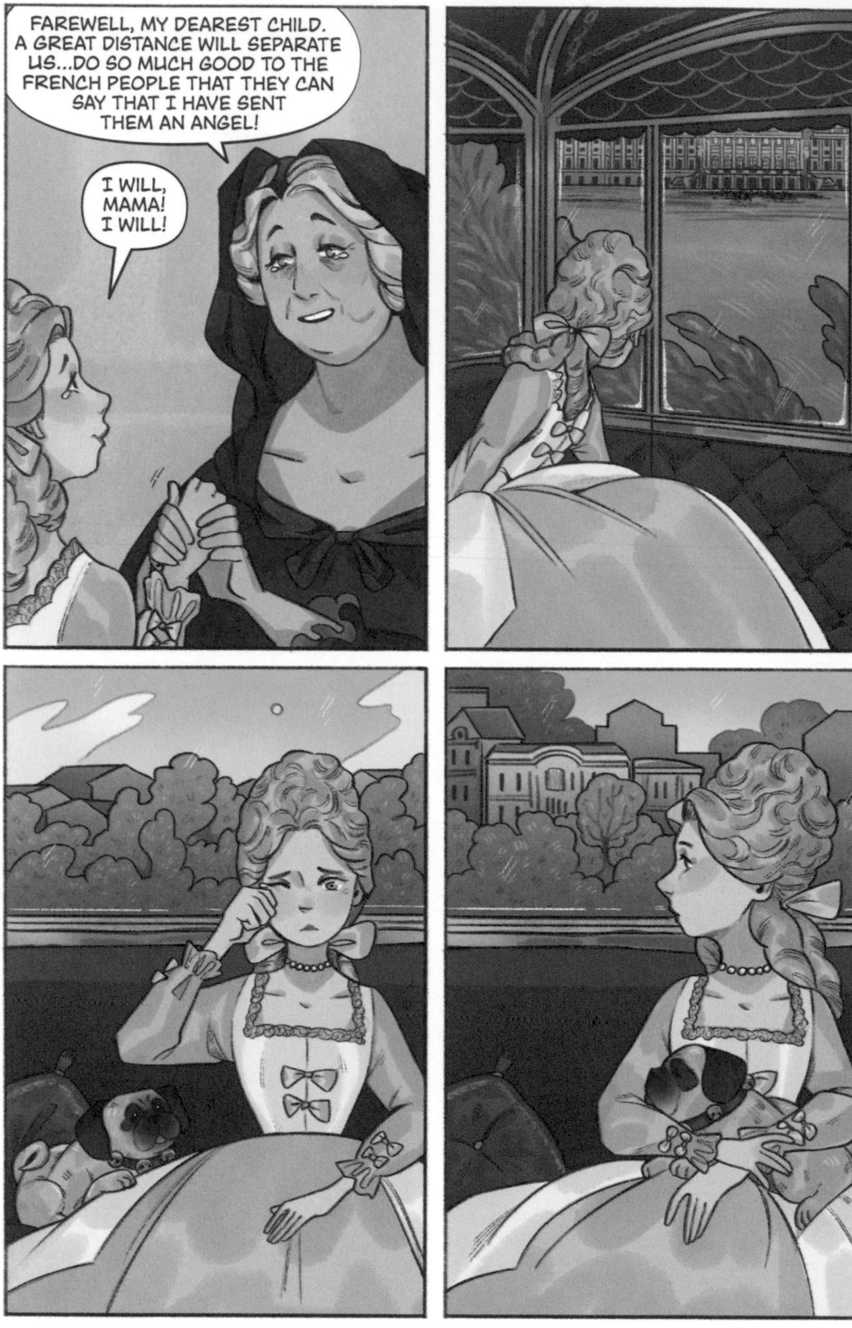
FAREWELL, MY DEAREST CHILD. A GREAT DISTANCE WILL SEPARATE US...DO SO MUCH GOOD TO THE FRENCH PEOPLE THAT THEY CAN SAY THAT I HAVE SENT THEM AN ANGEL!
I WILL, MAMA! I WILL!

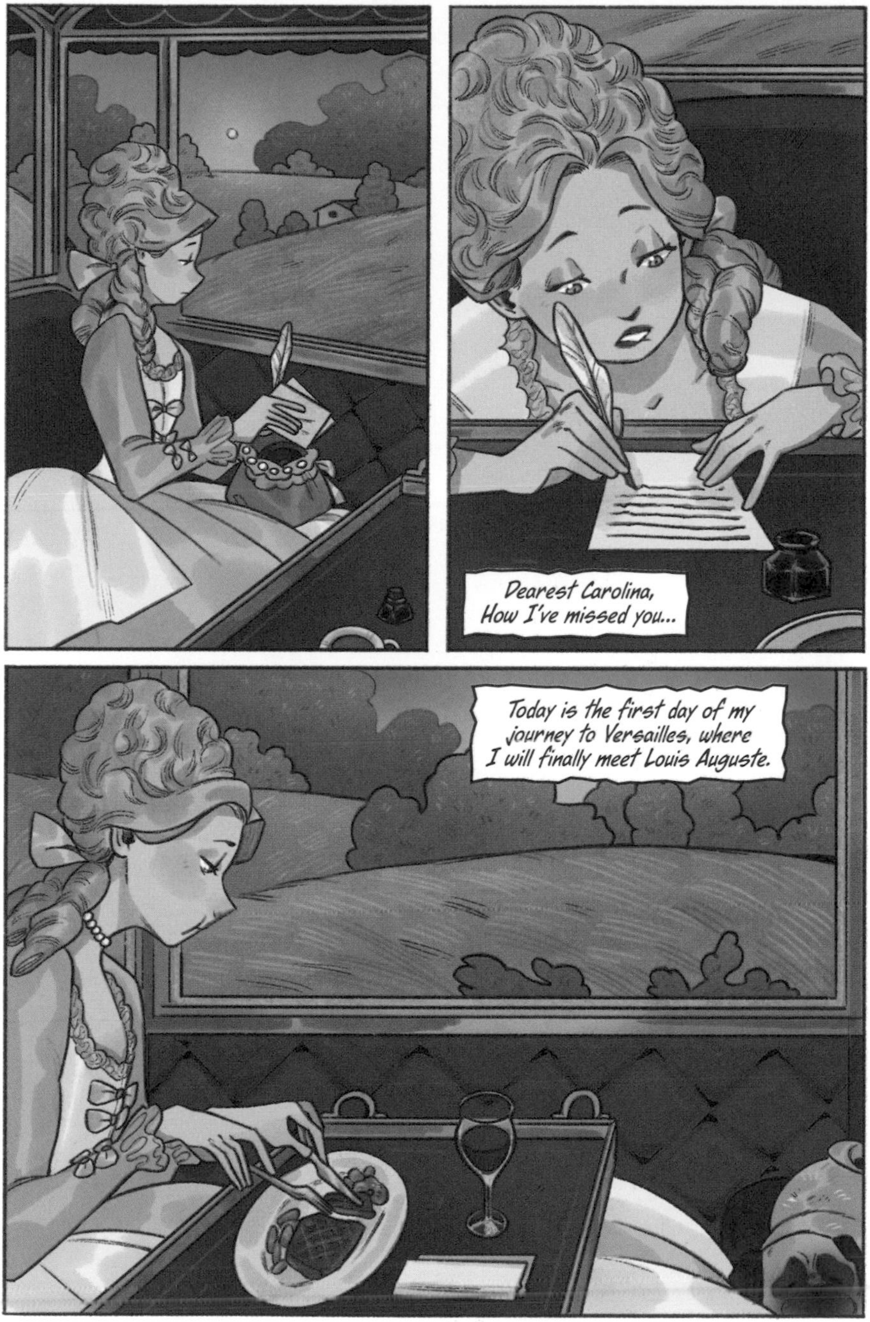
Dearest Carolina,
How I've missed you...
Today is the first day of my journey to Versailles, where I will finally meet Louis Auguste.

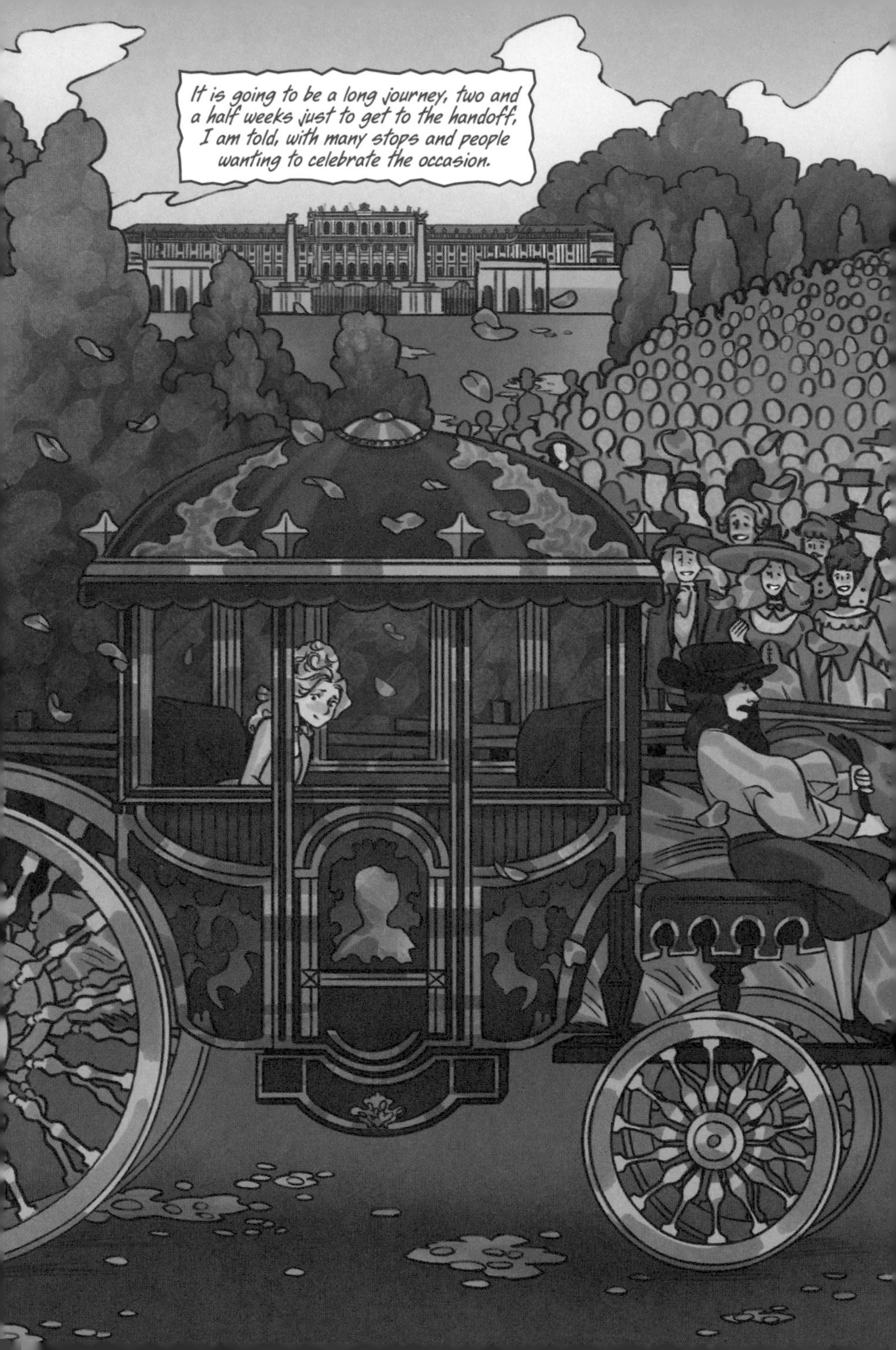
It is going to be a long journey, two and a half weeks just to get to the handoff, I am told, with many stops and people wanting to celebrate the occasion.

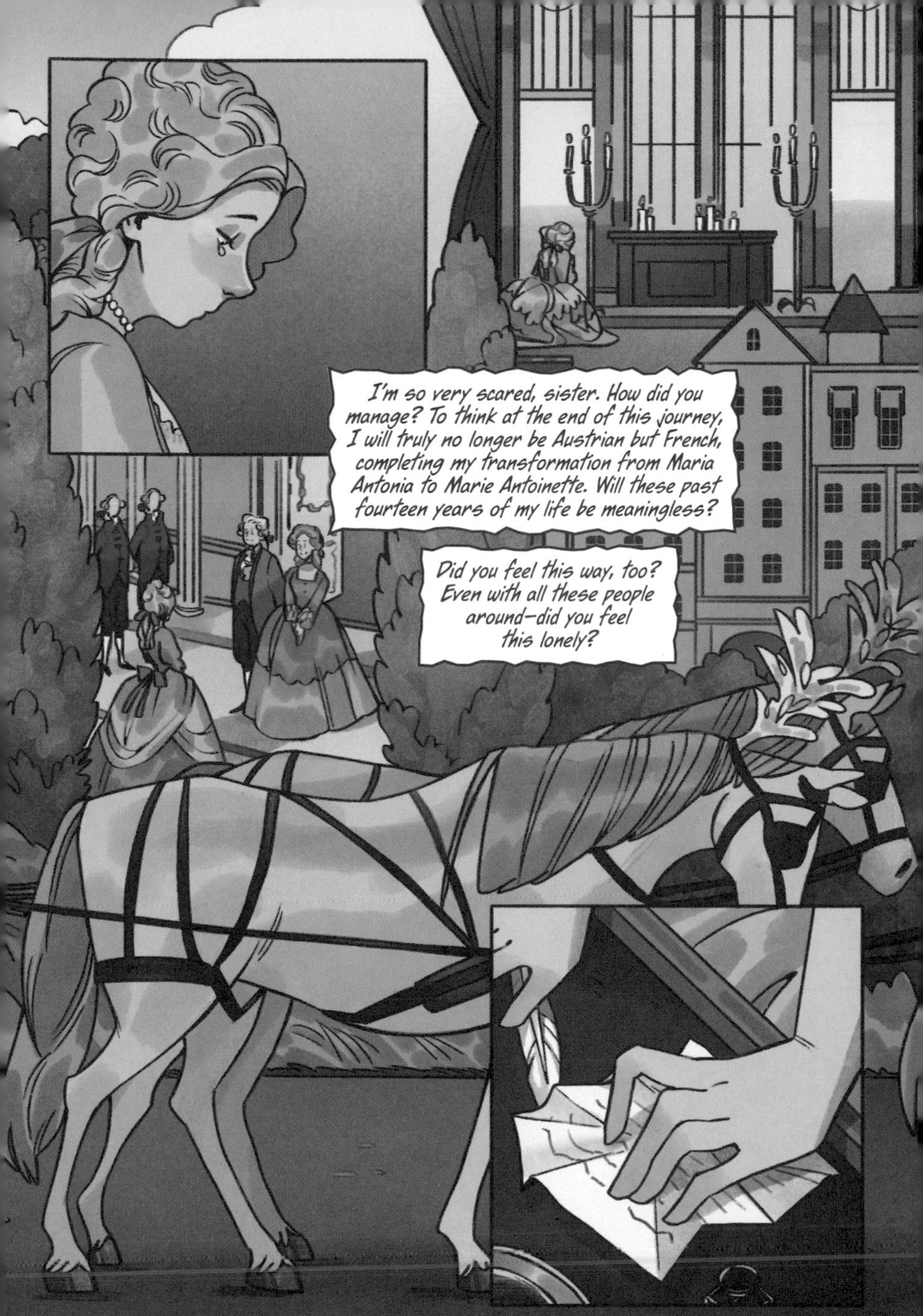
I'm so very scared, sister. How did you manage? To think at the end of this journey, I will truly no longer be Austrian but French, completing my transformation from Maria Antonia to Marie Antoinette. Will these past fourteen years of my life be meaningless?
Did you feel this way, too? Even with all these people around–did you feel this lonely?

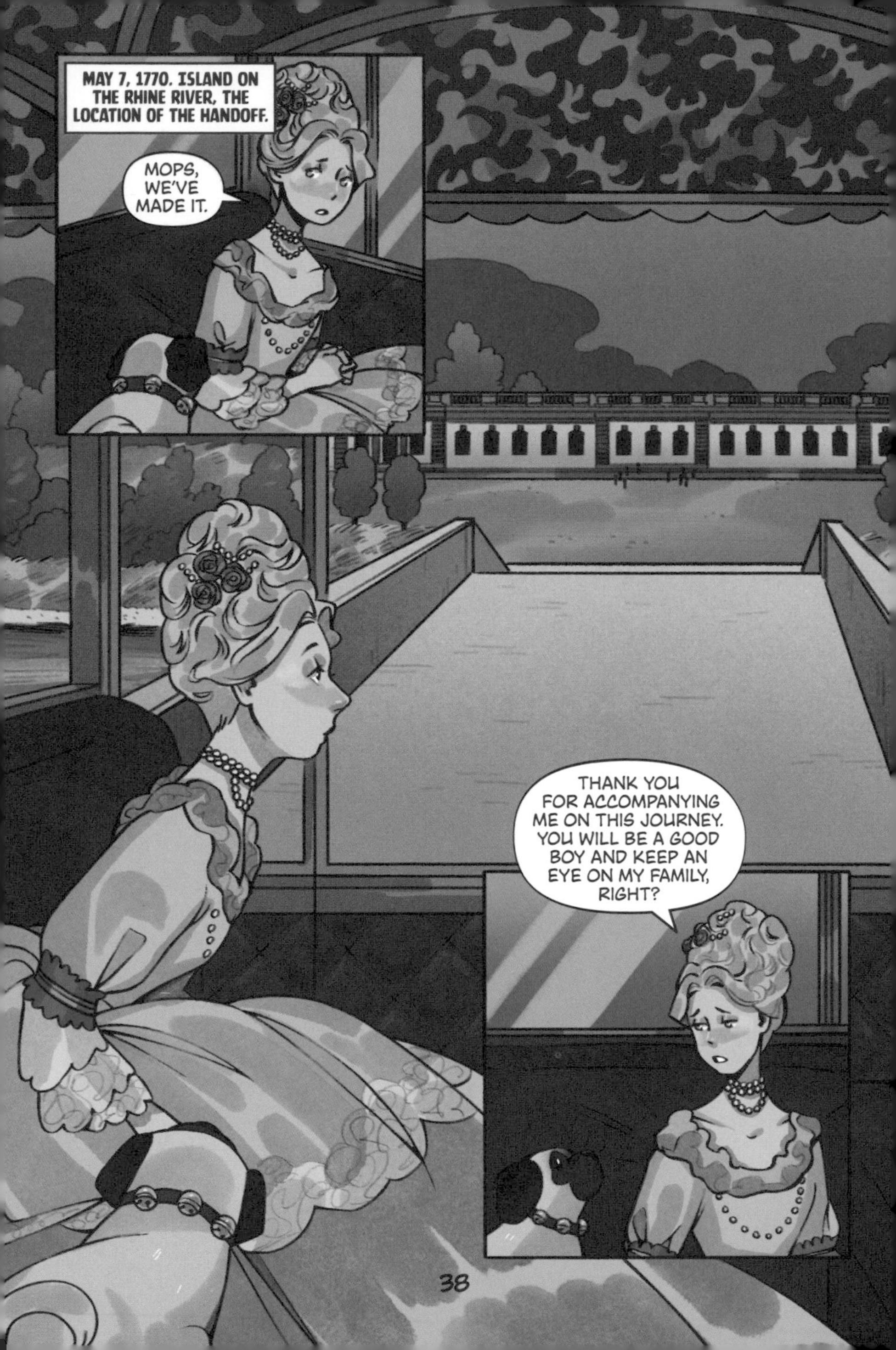
MAY 7, 1770. ISLAND ON THE RHINE RIVER, THE LOCATION OF THE HANDOFF.
MOPS, WE'VE MADE IT.
THANK YOU FOR ACCOMPANYING ME ON THIS JOURNEY. YOU WILL BE A GOOD BOY AND KEEP AN EYE ON MY FAMILY, RIGHT?

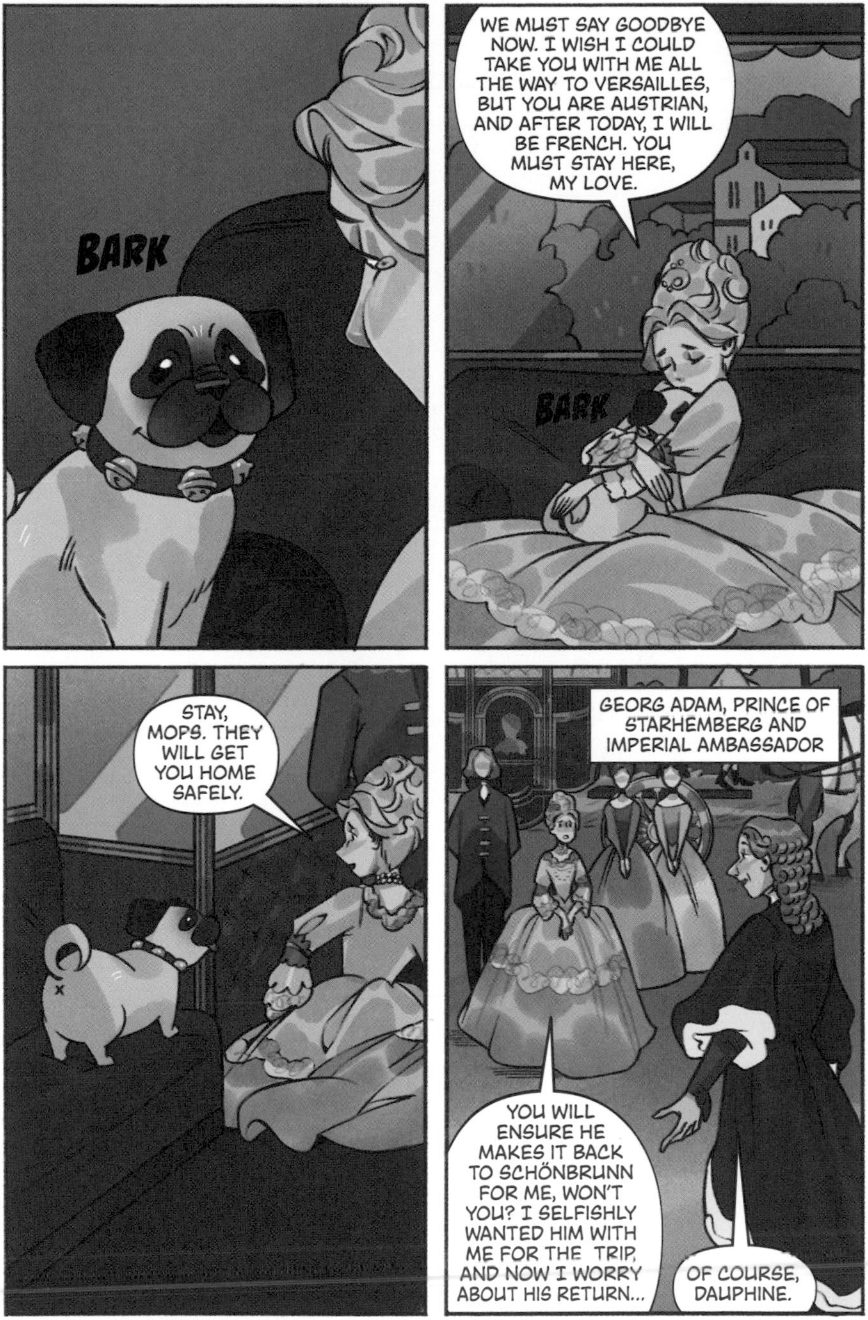
BARK
WE MUST SAY GOODBYE NOW. I WISH I COULD TAKE YOU WITH ME ALL THE WAY TO VERSAILLES, BUT YOU ARE AUSTRIAN, AND AFTER TODAY, I WILL BE FRENCH. YOU MUST STAY HERE, MY LOVE.
BARK
STAY, MOPS. THEY WILL GET YOU HOME SAFELY.
GEORG ADAM, PRINCE OF STARHEMBERG AND IMPERIAL AMBASSADOR
YOU WILL ENSURE HE MAKES IT BACK TO SCHÖNBRUNN FOR ME, WON'T YOU? I SELFISHLY WANTED HIM WITH ME FOR THE TRIP, AND NOW I WORRY ABOUT HIS RETURN...
OF COURSE, DAUPHINE.

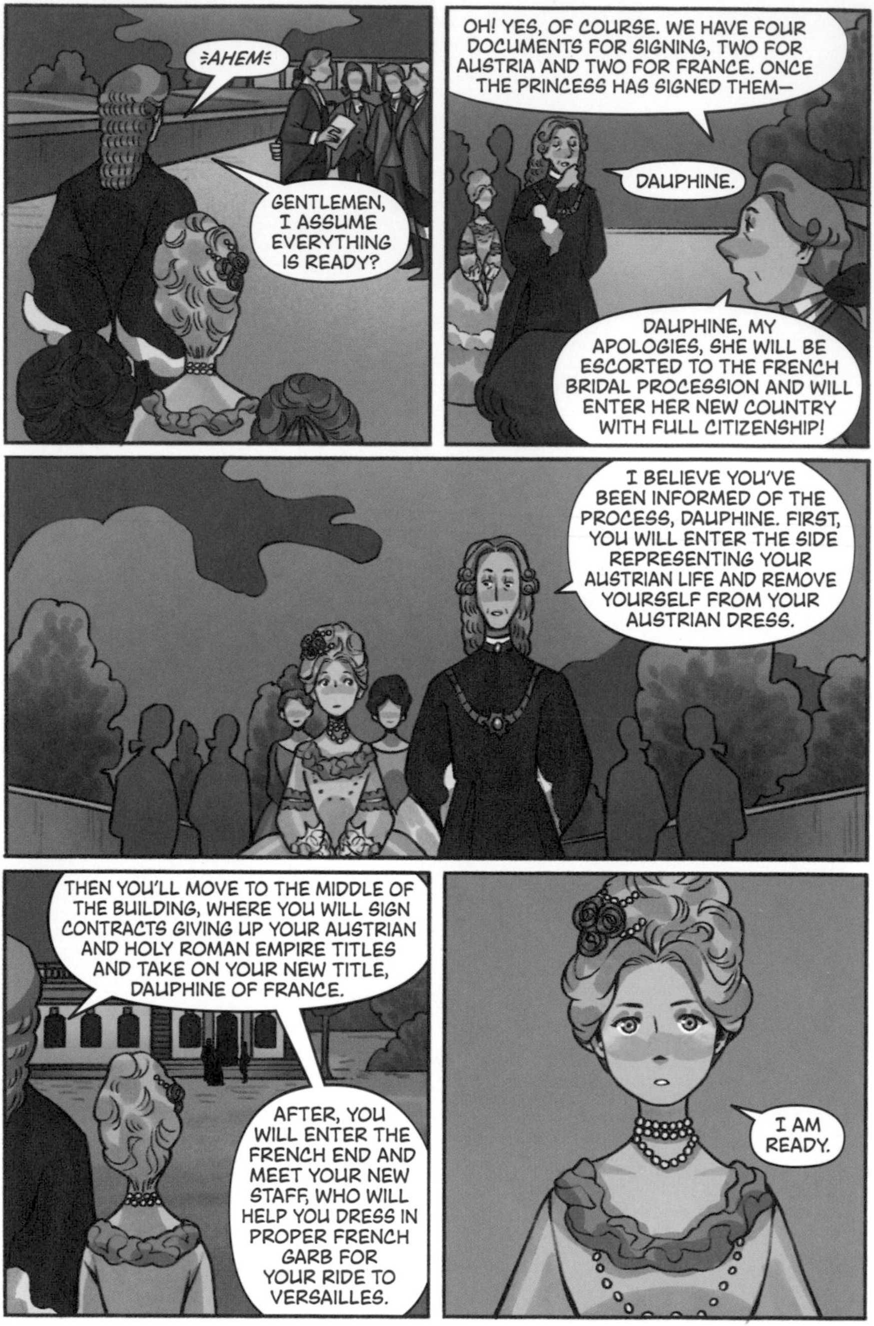
AHEM
GENTLEMEN, I ASSUME EVERYTHING IS READY?
OH! YES, OF COURSE. WE HAVE FOUR DOCUMENTS FOR SIGNING, TWO FOR AUSTRIA AND TWO FOR FRANCE. ONCE THE PRINCESS HAS SIGNED THEM—
DAUPHINE.
DAUPHINE, MY APOLOGIES, SHE WILL BE ESCORTED TO THE FRENCH BRIDAL PROCESSION AND WILL ENTER HER NEW COUNTRY WITH FULL CITIZENSHIP!
I BELIEVE YOU'VE BEEN INFORMED OF THE PROCESS, DAUPHINE. FIRST, YOU WILL ENTER THE SIDE REPRESENTING YOUR AUSTRIAN LIFE AND REMOVE YOURSELF FROM YOUR AUSTRIAN DRESS.
THEN YOU'LL MOVE TO THE MIDDLE OF THE BUILDING, WHERE YOU WILL SIGN CONTRACTS GIVING UP YOUR AUSTRIAN AND HOLY ROMAN EMPIRE TITLES AND TAKE ON YOUR NEW TITLE, DAUPHINE OF FRANCE.
AFTER, YOU WILL ENTER THE FRENCH END AND MEET YOUR NEW STAFF, WHO WILL HELP YOU DRESS IN PROPER FRENCH GARB FOR YOUR RIDE TO VERSAILLES.
I AM READY.

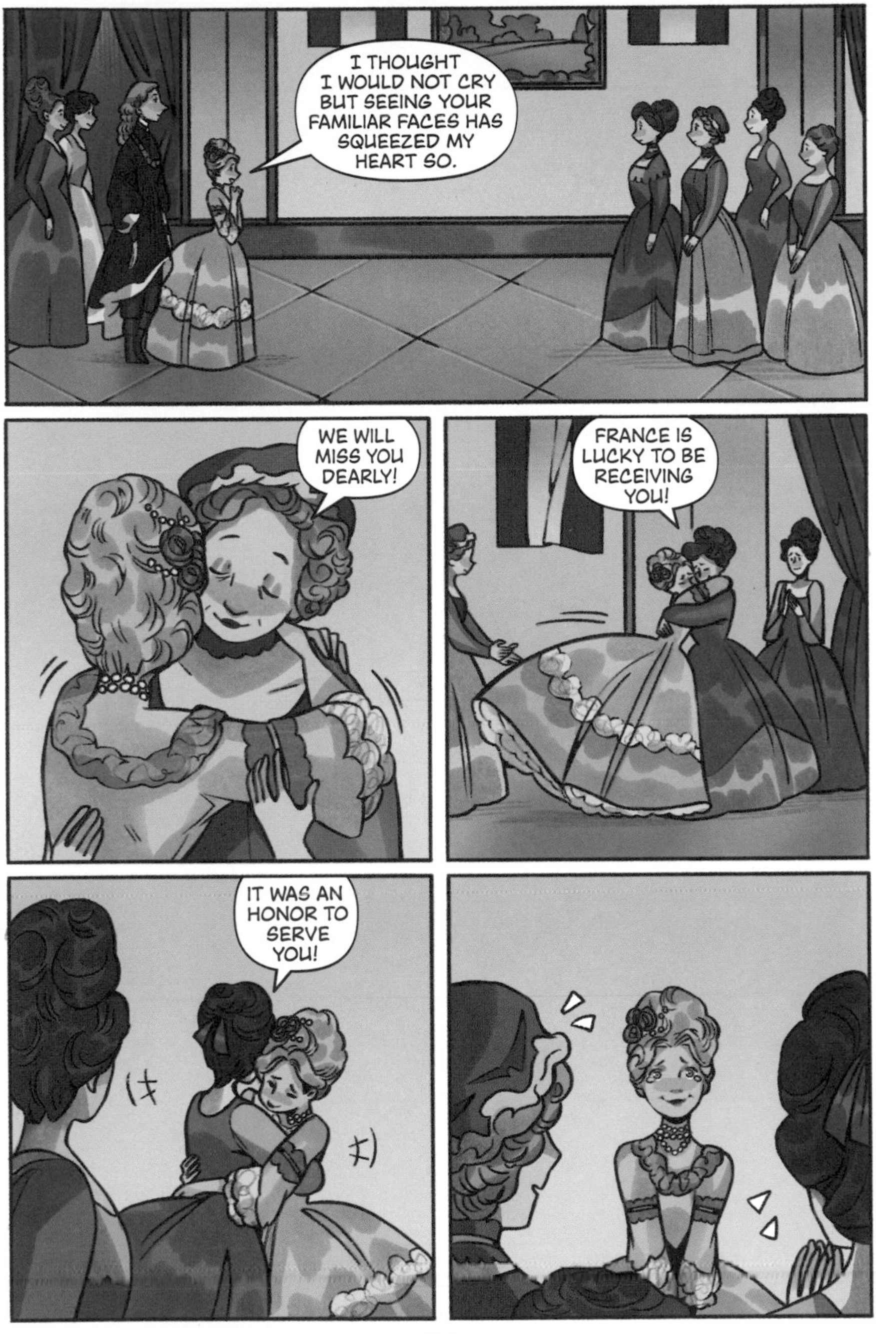
I THOUGHT I WOULD NOT CRY BUT SEEING YOUR FAMILIAR FACES HAS SQUEEZED MY HEART SO.
WE WILL MISS YOU DEARLY!
FRANCE IS LUCKY TO BE RECEIVING YOU!
IT WAS AN HONOR TO SERVE YOU!

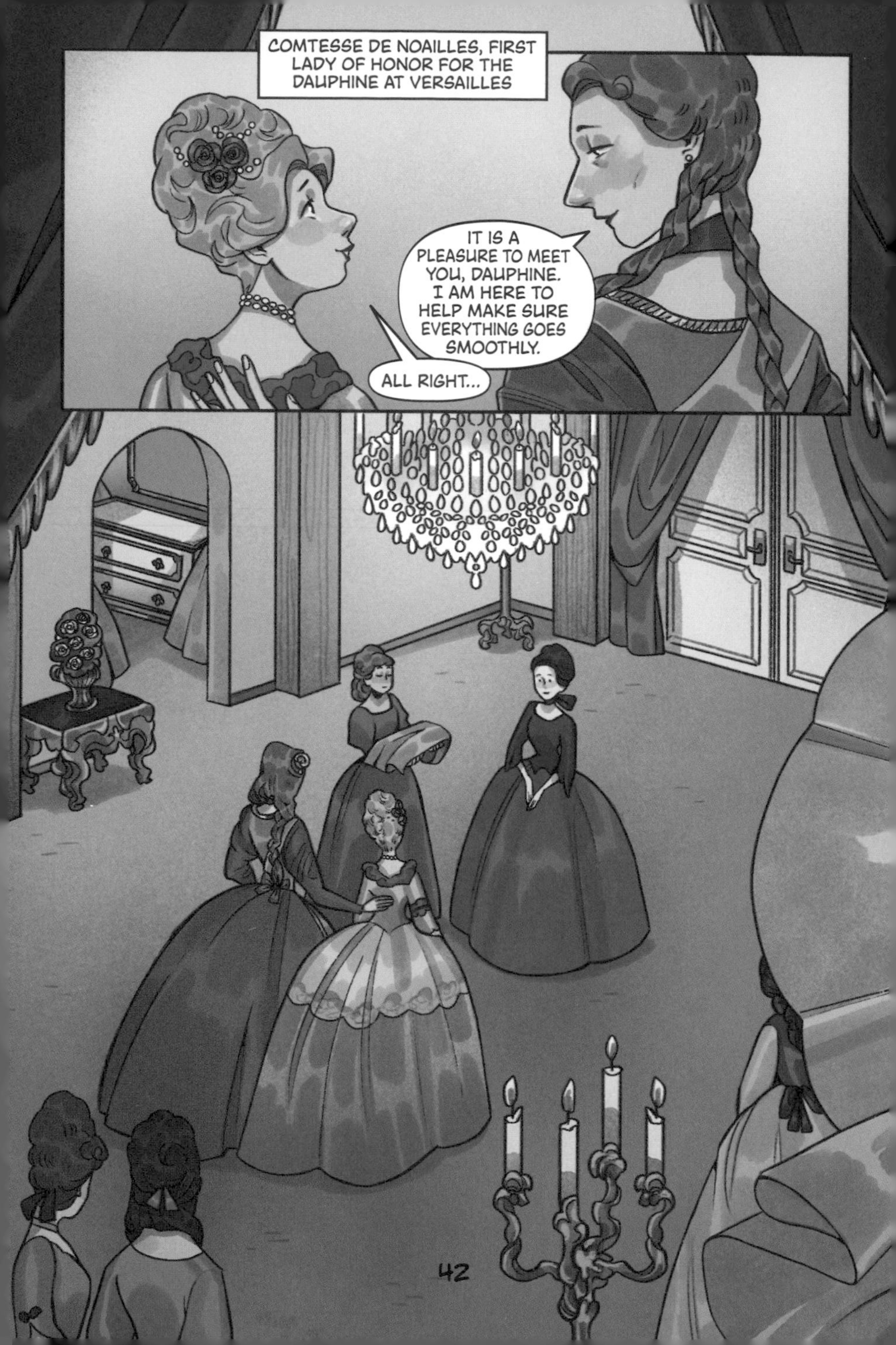
COMTESSE DE NOAILLES, FIRST LADY OF HONOR FOR THE DAUPHINE AT VERSAILLES
IT IS A PLEASURE TO MEET YOU, DAUPHINE. I AM HERE TO HELP MAKE SURE EVERYTHING GOES SMOOTHLY.
ALL RIGHT...

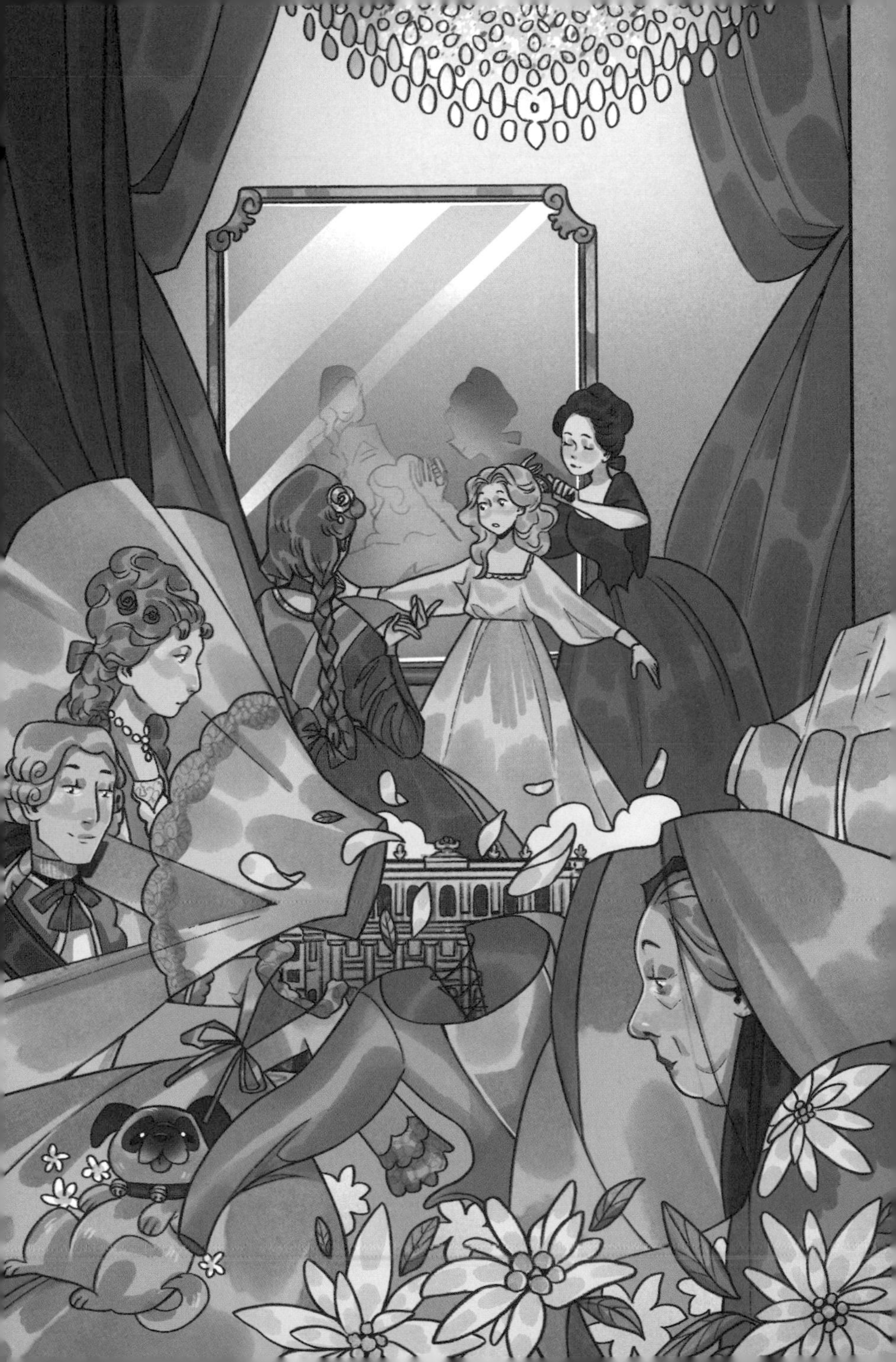

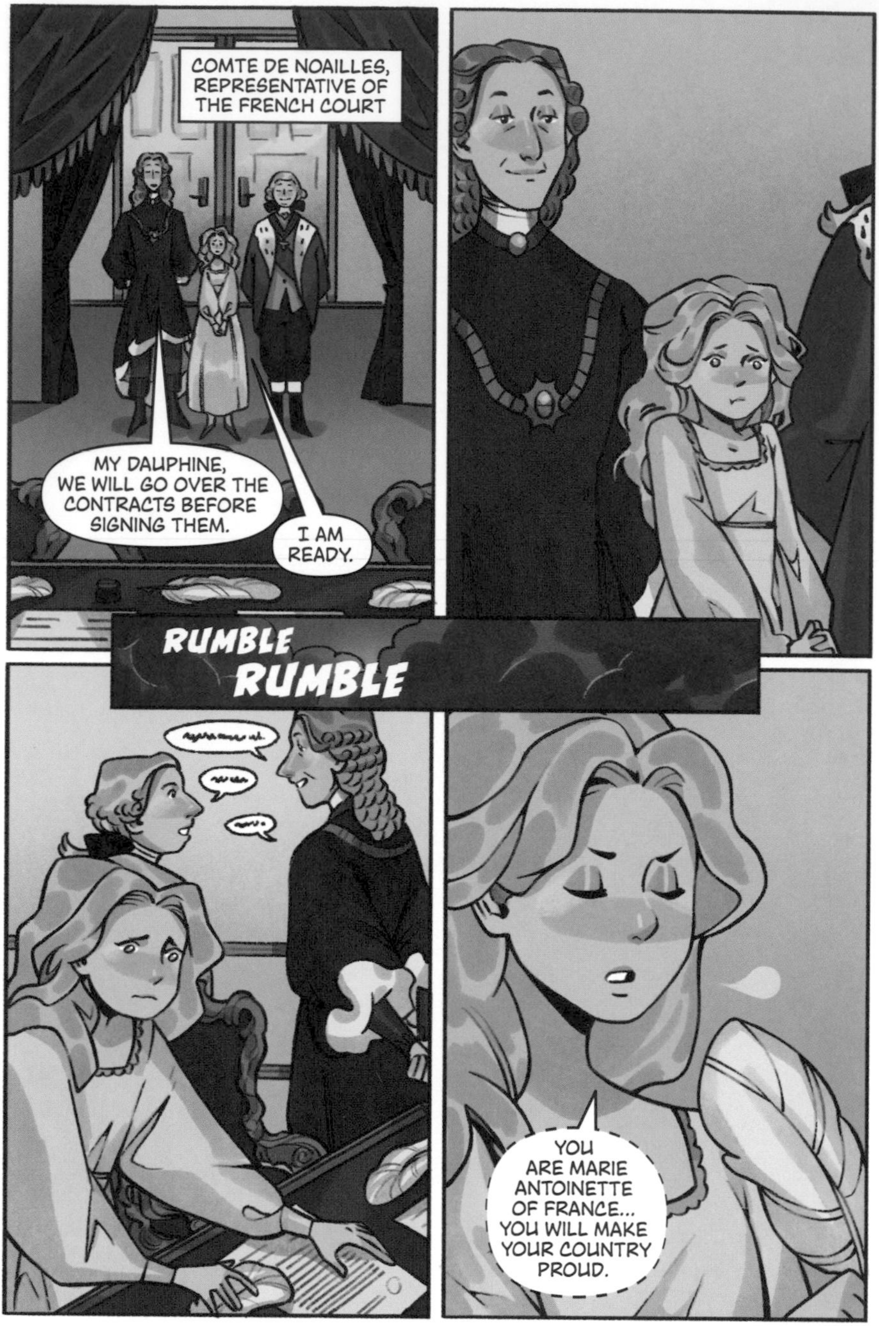
COMTE DE NOAILLES, REPRESENTATIVE OF THE FRENCH COURT
MY DAUPHINE, WE WILL GO OVER THE CONTRACTS BEFORE SIGNING THEM.
I AM READY.
RUMBLE RUMBLE
YOU ARE MARIE ANTOINETTE OF FRANCE... YOU WILL MAKE YOUR COUNTRY PROUD.

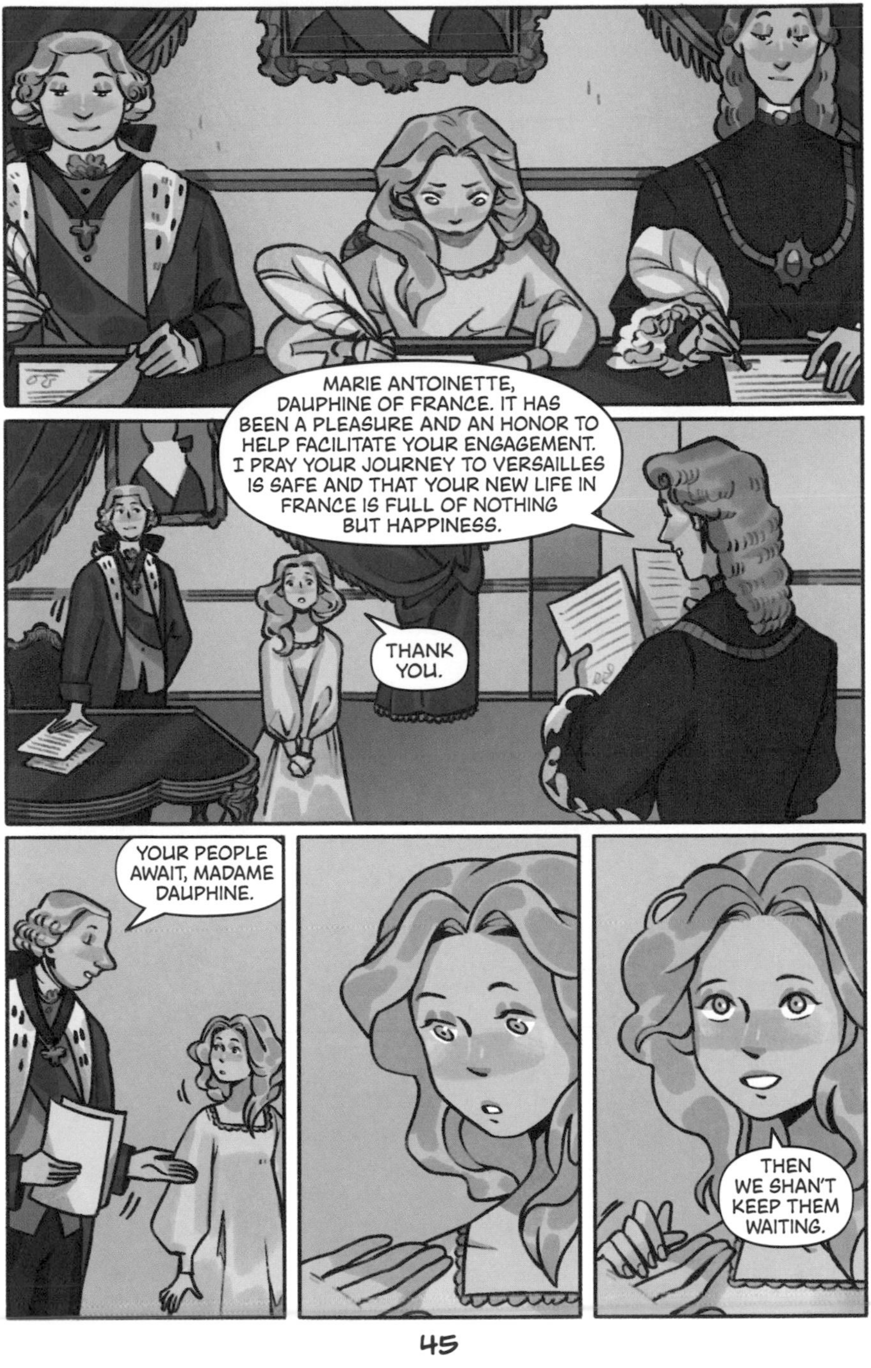
MARIE ANTOINETTE, DAUPHINE OF FRANCE. IT HAS BEEN A PLEASURE AND AN HONOR TO HELP FACILITATE YOUR ENGAGEMENT. I PRAY YOUR JOURNEY TO VERSAILLES IS SAFE AND THAT YOUR NEW LIFE IN FRANCE IS FULL OF NOTHING BUT HAPPINESS.
THANK YOU.
YOUR PEOPLE AWAIT, MADAME DAUPHINE.
THEN WE SHAN'T KEEP THEM WAITING.

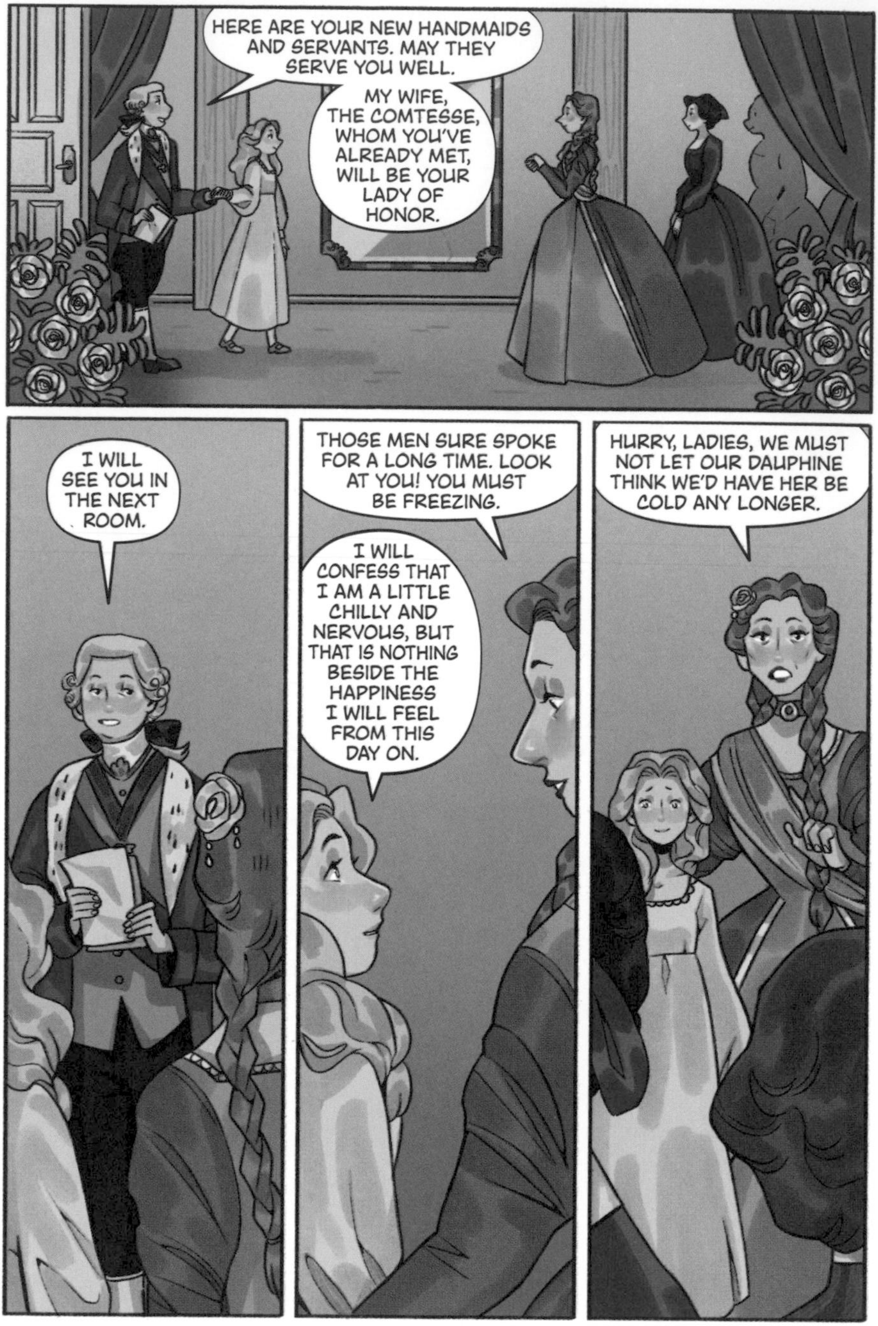
HERE ARE YOUR NEW HANDMAIDS AND SERVANTS. MAY THEY SERVE YOU WELL.
MY WIFE, THE COMTESSE, WHOM YOU'VE ALREADY MET, WILL BE YOUR LADY OF HONOR.
I WILL SEE YOU IN THE NEXT ROOM.
THOSE MEN SURE SPOKE FOR A LONG TIME. LOOK AT YOU! YOU MUST BE FREEZING.
I WILL CONFESS THAT I AM A LITTLE CHILLY AND NERVOUS, BUT THAT IS NOTHING BESIDE THE HAPPINESS I WILL FEEL FROM THIS DAY ON.
HURRY, LADIES, WE MUST NOT LET OUR DAUPHINE THINK WE'D HAVE HER BE COLD ANY LONGER.

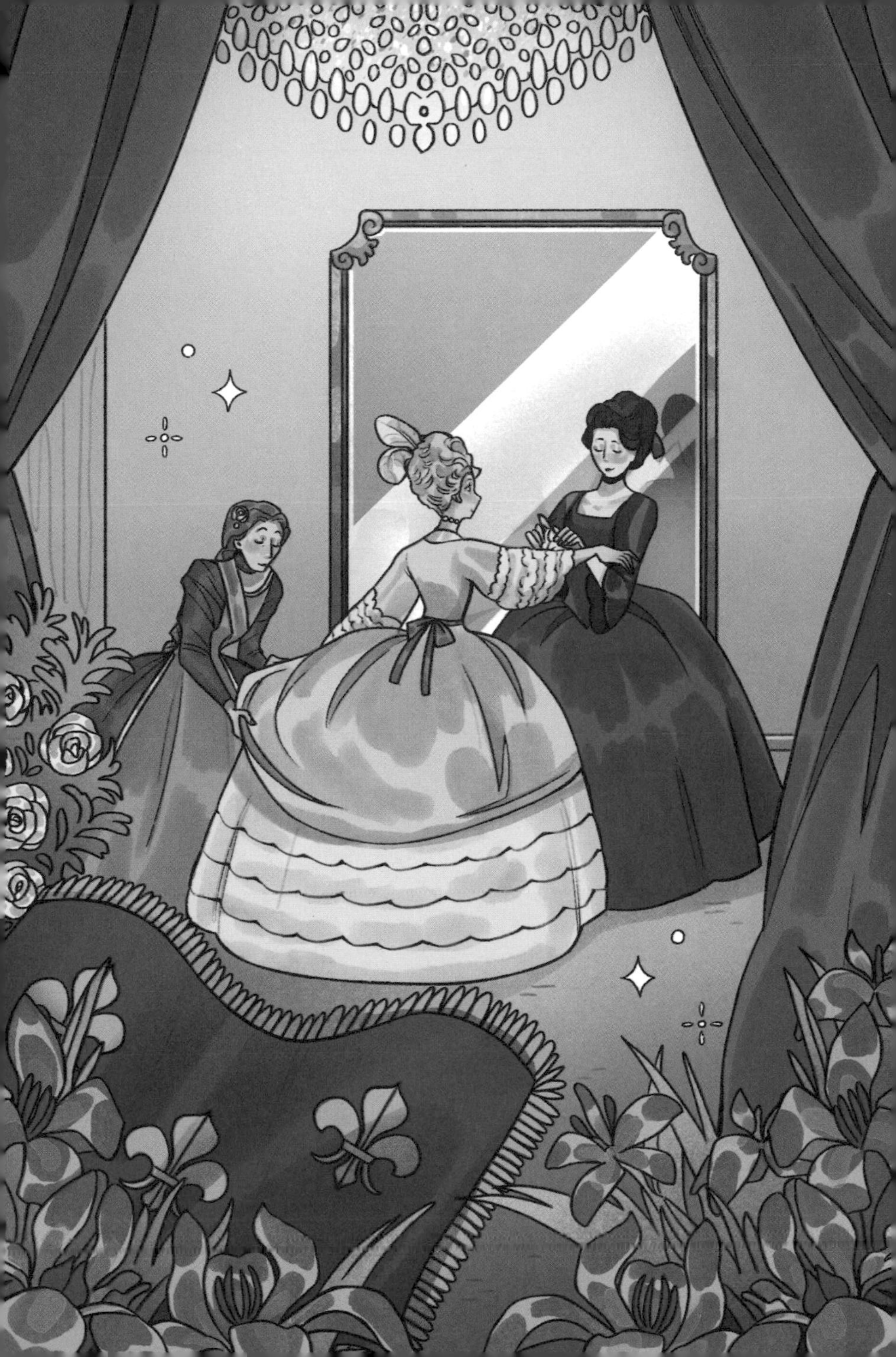

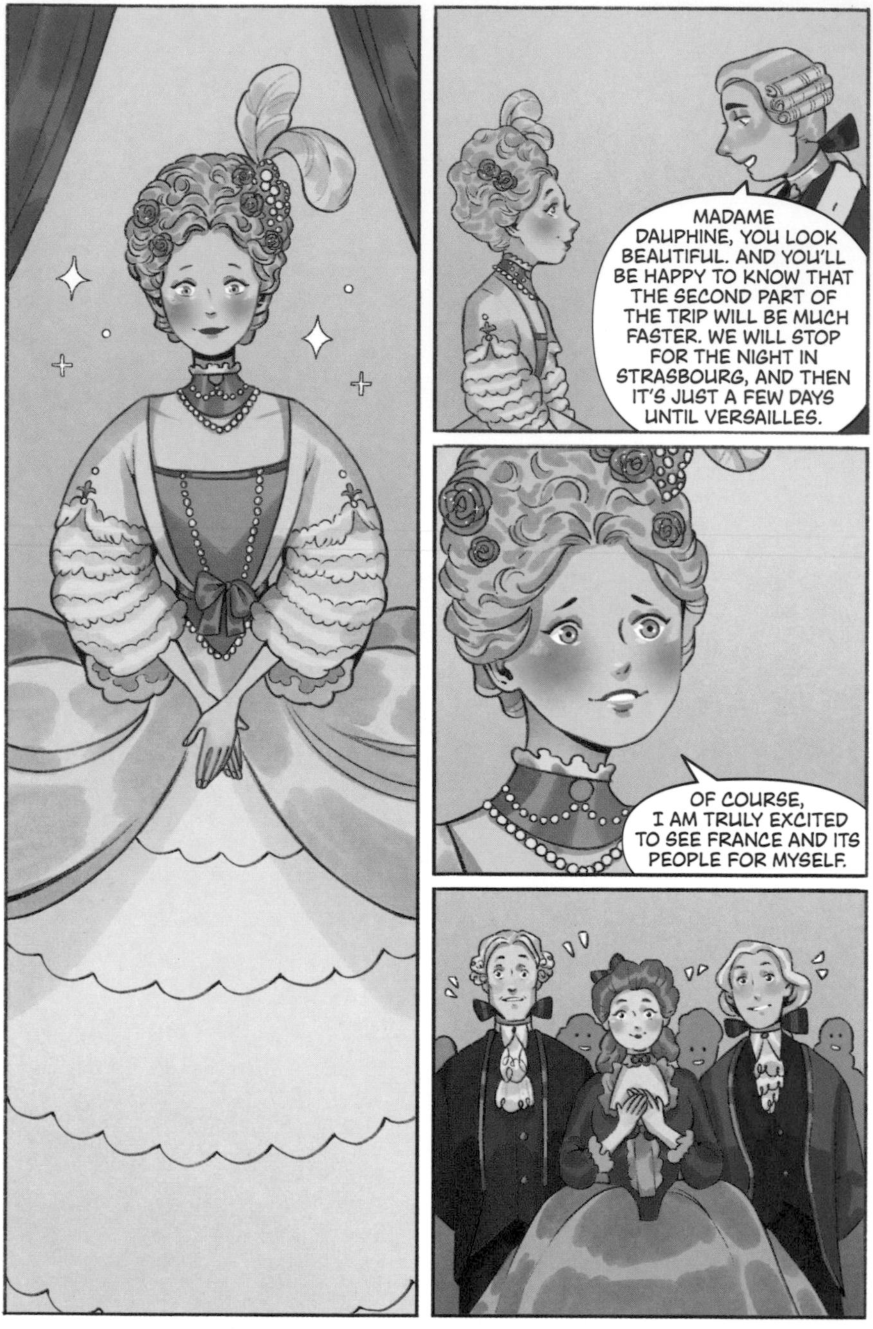
MADAME DAUPHINE, YOU LOOK BEAUTIFUL. AND YOU'LL BE HAPPY TO KNOW THAT THE SECOND PART OF THE TRIP WILL BE MUCH FASTER. WE WILL STOP FOR THE NIGHT IN STRASBOURG, AND THEN IT'S JUST A FEW DAYS UNTIL VERSAILLES.
OF COURSE, I AM TRULY EXCITED TO SEE FRANCE AND ITS PEOPLE FOR MYSELF.

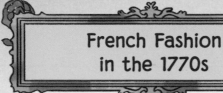

When fourteen-year-old Marie Antoinette first arrived at the Palace of Versailles, fashion was already very important to the French court. She didn't know then that she would become a fashion icon infamous for her frivolous spending. In Versailles, she had entire rooms dedicated to her wardrobe and even a book with swathes of cloth matching each of her outfits so that she could choose what to wear every morning before getting out of bed.

The most notable style Marie Antoinette became famous for wasn't something she invented, but she certainly made it popular: the pouf, a large headdress made from real and fake hair that was framed with metal bars and highly decorated to tell stories. After a French win in the seas, Marie Antoinette wore a pouf with a French warship to celebrate.

French style had an influence on Marie Antoinette as well, who grew fond of putting rouge on her cheeks—something her eldest brother made fun of her for during his visit to court.

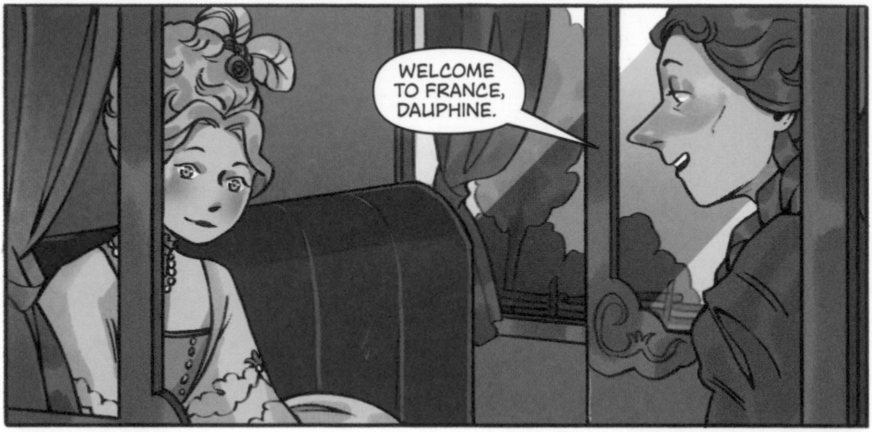
WELCOME TO FRANCE, DAUPHINE.

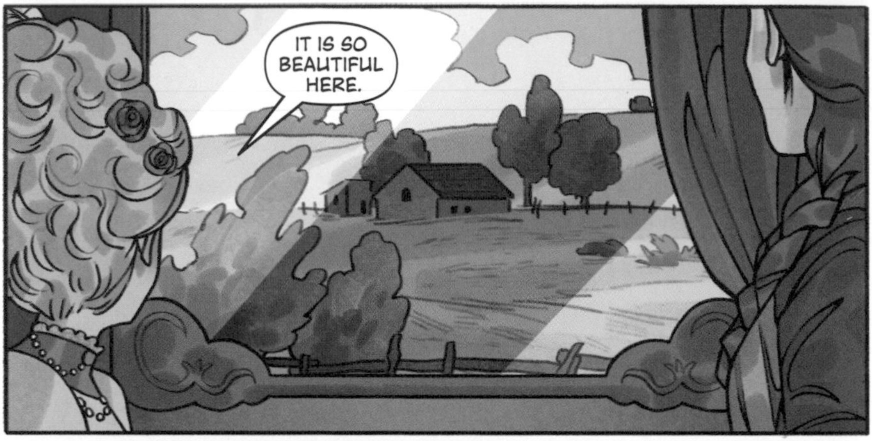
IT IS SO BEAUTIFUL HERE.

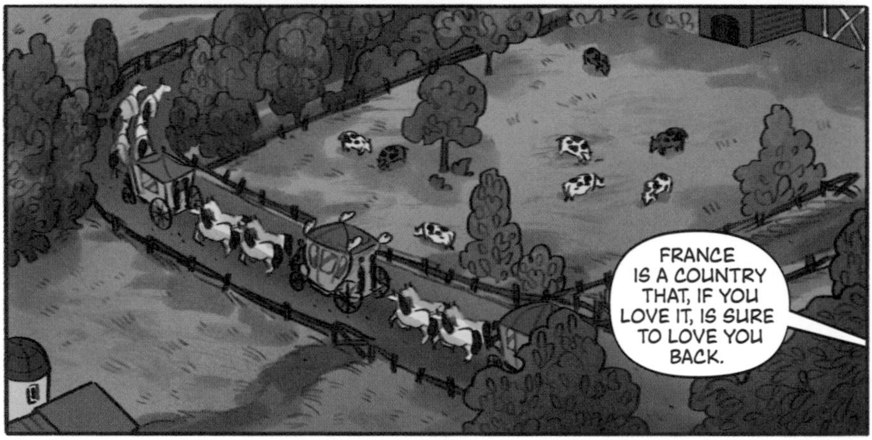
FRANCE IS A COUNTRY THAT, IF YOU LOVE IT, IS SURE TO LOVE YOU BACK.

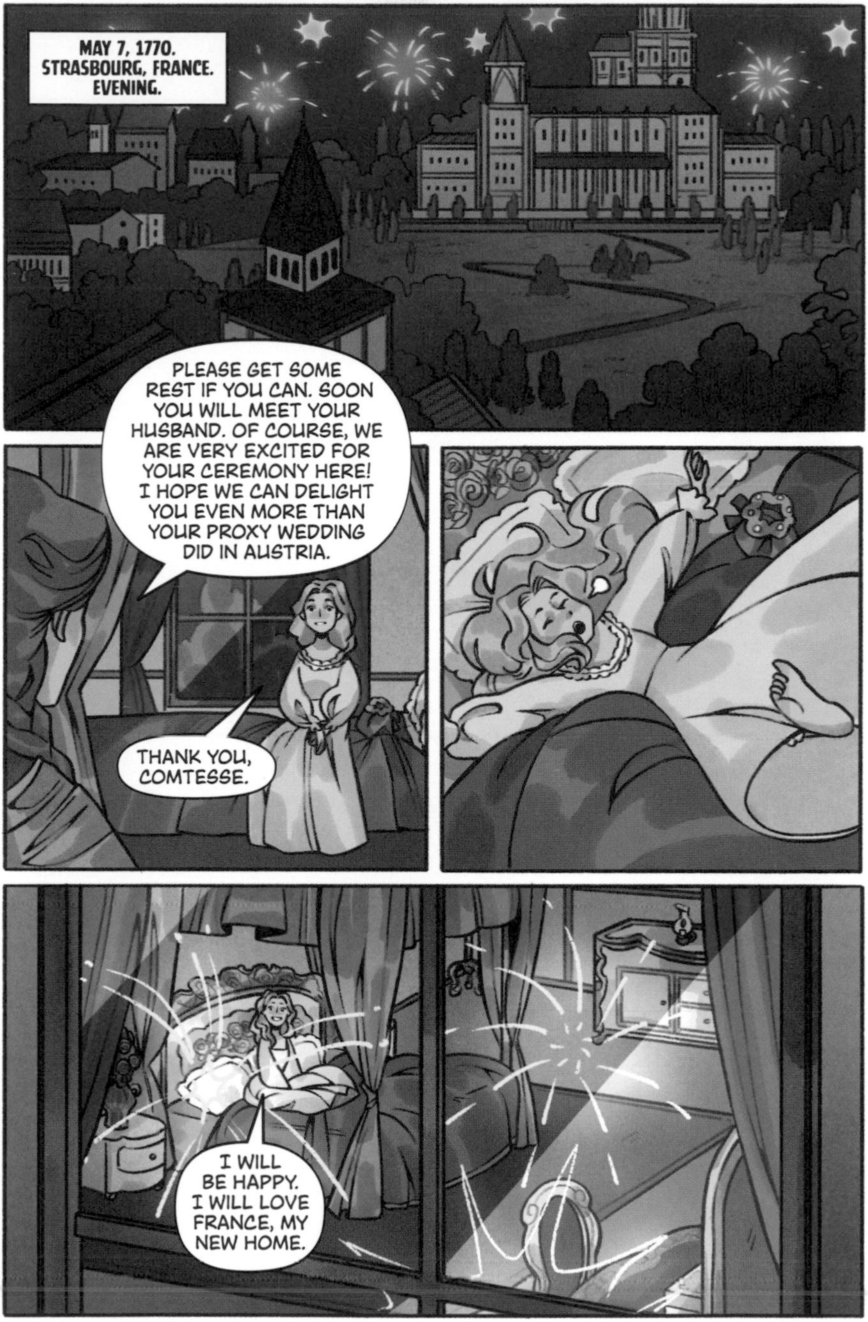
MAY 7, 1770. STRASBOURG, FRANCE. EVENING.
PLEASE GET SOME REST IF YOU CAN. SOON YOU WILL MEET YOUR HUSBAND. OF COURSE, WE ARE VERY EXCITED FOR YOUR CEREMONY HERE! I HOPE WE CAN DELIGHT YOU EVEN MORE THAN YOUR PROXY WEDDING DID IN AUSTRIA.
THANK YOU, COMTESSE.
I WILL BE HAPPY. I WILL LOVE FRANCE, MY NEW HOME.

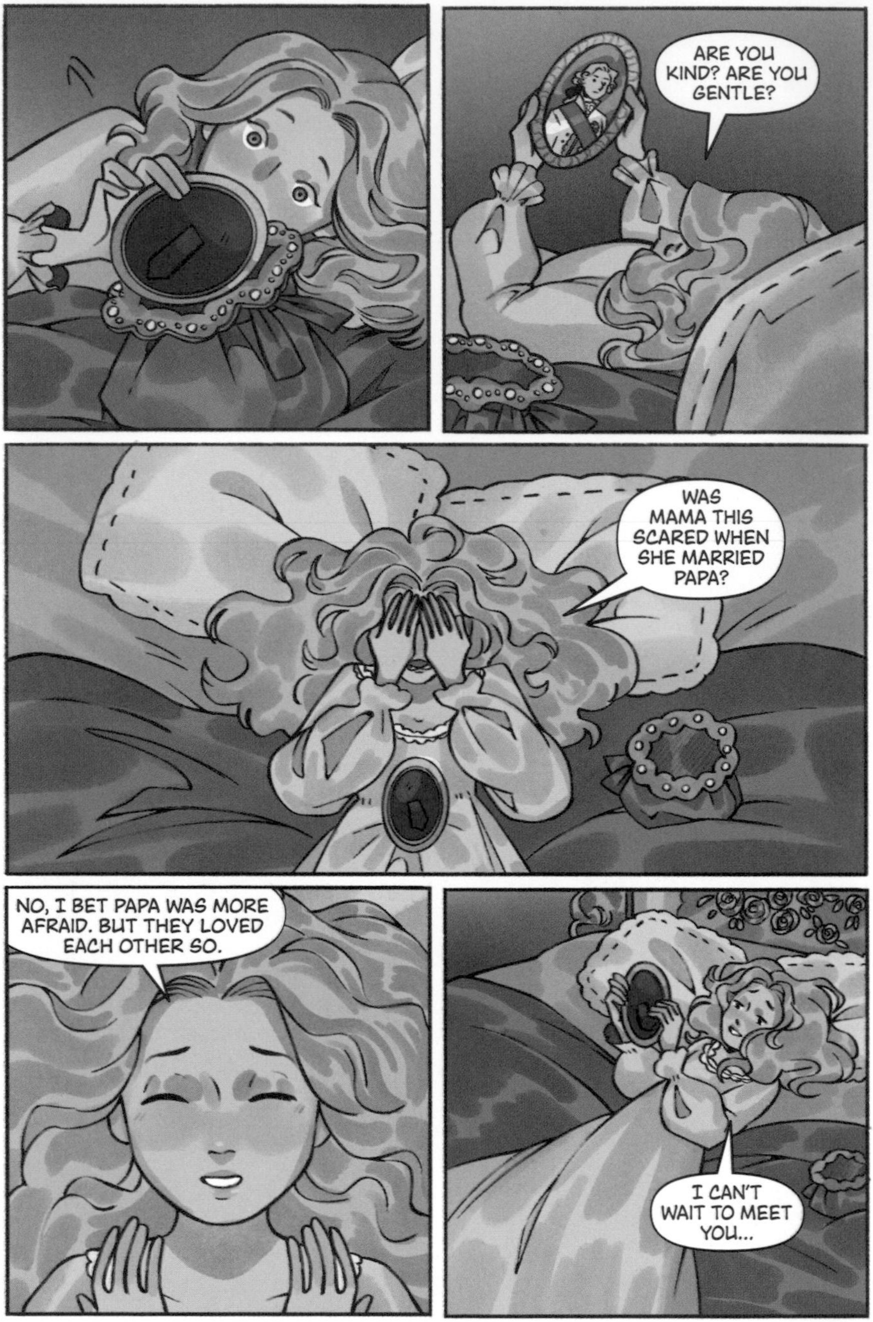
ARE YOU KIND? ARE YOU GENTLE?
WAS MAMA THIS SCARED WHEN SHE MARRIED PAPA?
NO, I BET PAPA WAS MORE AFRAID. BUT THEY LOVED EACH OTHER SO.
I CAN'T WAIT TO MEET YOU...

Louis XVI

Louis Auguste was born on August 23, 1754, at the Palace of Versailles. Much like Marie Antoinette, in his early years, Louis Auguste was overlooked by his parents, who spent their time with Louis's older brother. Though highly regarded, his brother died at the age of nine in 1761. Louis himself was a shy but smart child, good at his studies, which included Latin, history, geography, and astronomy. However, Louis's studies did not shape him into becoming a good king; in fact, he was known for being indecisive, for which many historians blame his instructors.

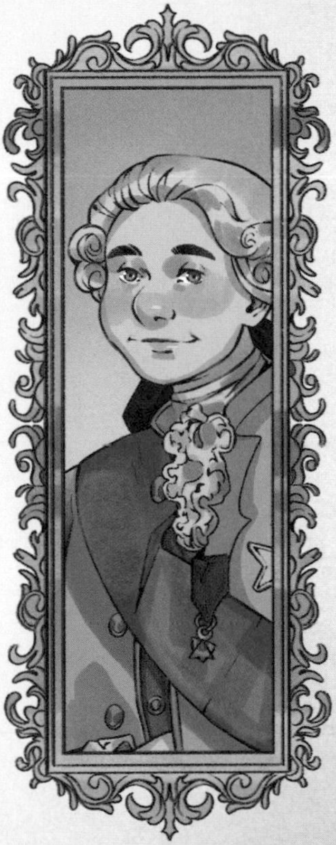

After Louis's father died in 1765, Louis became the dauphin and heir apparent for the French crown. Louis Auguste first met Marie Antoinette at age fifteen, and the two teenagers got off to an unsteady start as they adjusted to being a royal married couple, but eventually they were known to be extremely in love. They had four children who survived childbirth and four adopted children.

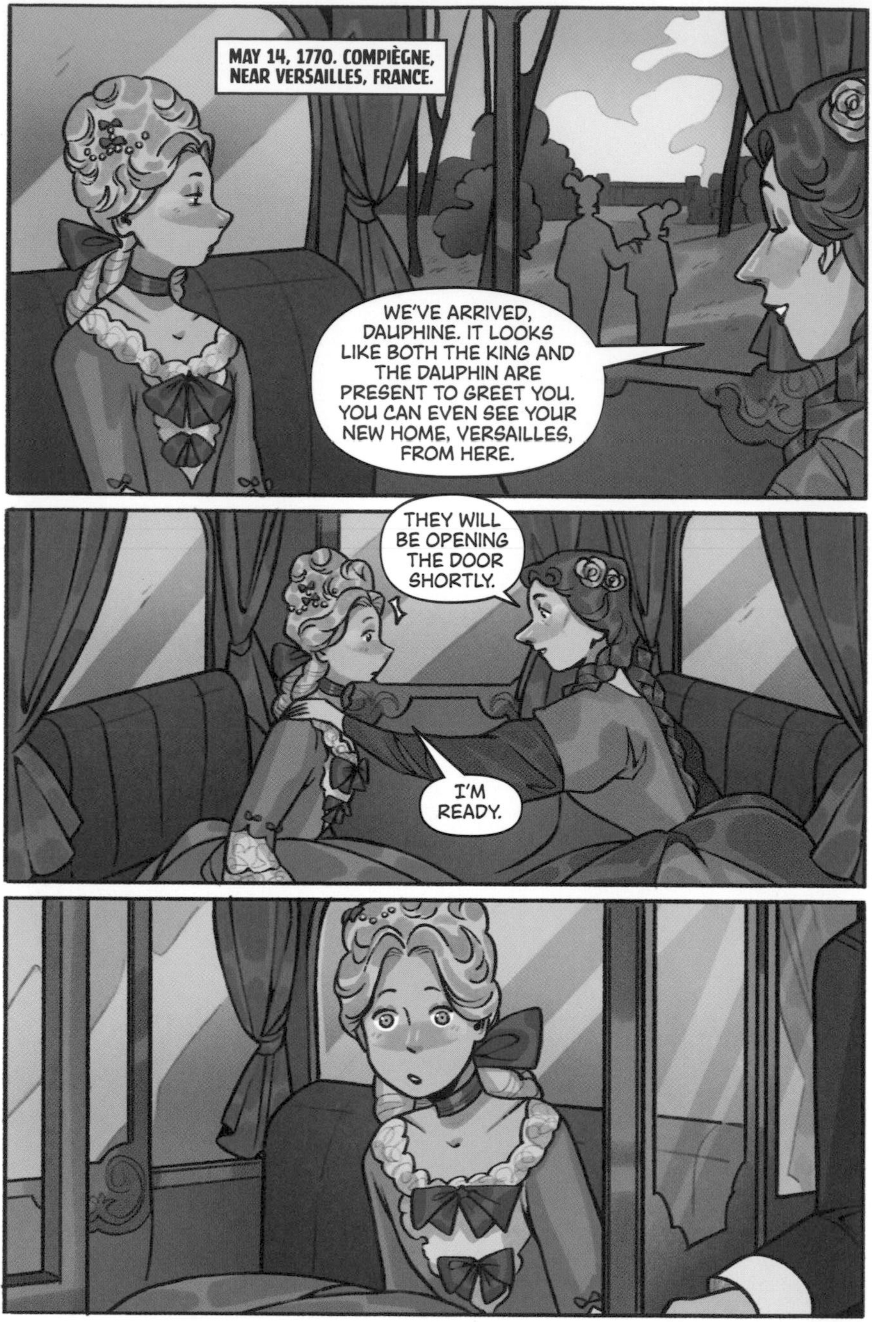
MAY 14, 1770. COMPIÈGNE, NEAR VERSAILLES, FRANCE.
WE'VE ARRIVED, DAUPHINE. IT LOOKS LIKE BOTH THE KING AND THE DAUPHIN ARE PRESENT TO GREET YOU. YOU CAN EVEN SEE YOUR NEW HOME, VERSAILLES, FROM HERE.
THEY WILL BE OPENING THE DOOR SHORTLY.
I'M READY.

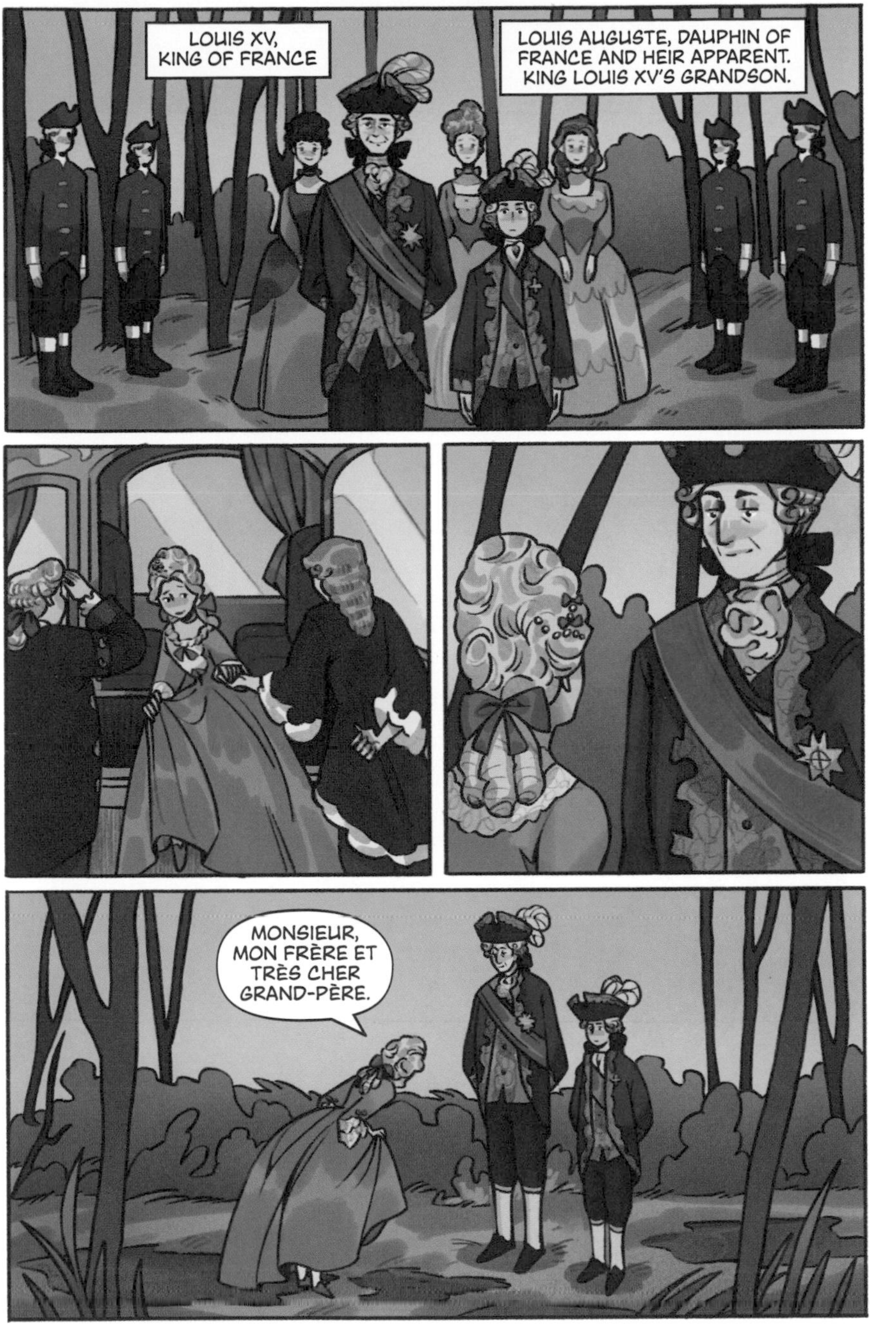
LOUIS XV, KING OF FRANCE
LOUIS AUGUSTE, DAUPHIN OF FRANCE AND HEIR APPARENT. KING LOUIS XV'S GRANDSON.
MONSIEUR, MON FRÈRE ET TRÈS CHER GRAND-PÈRE.

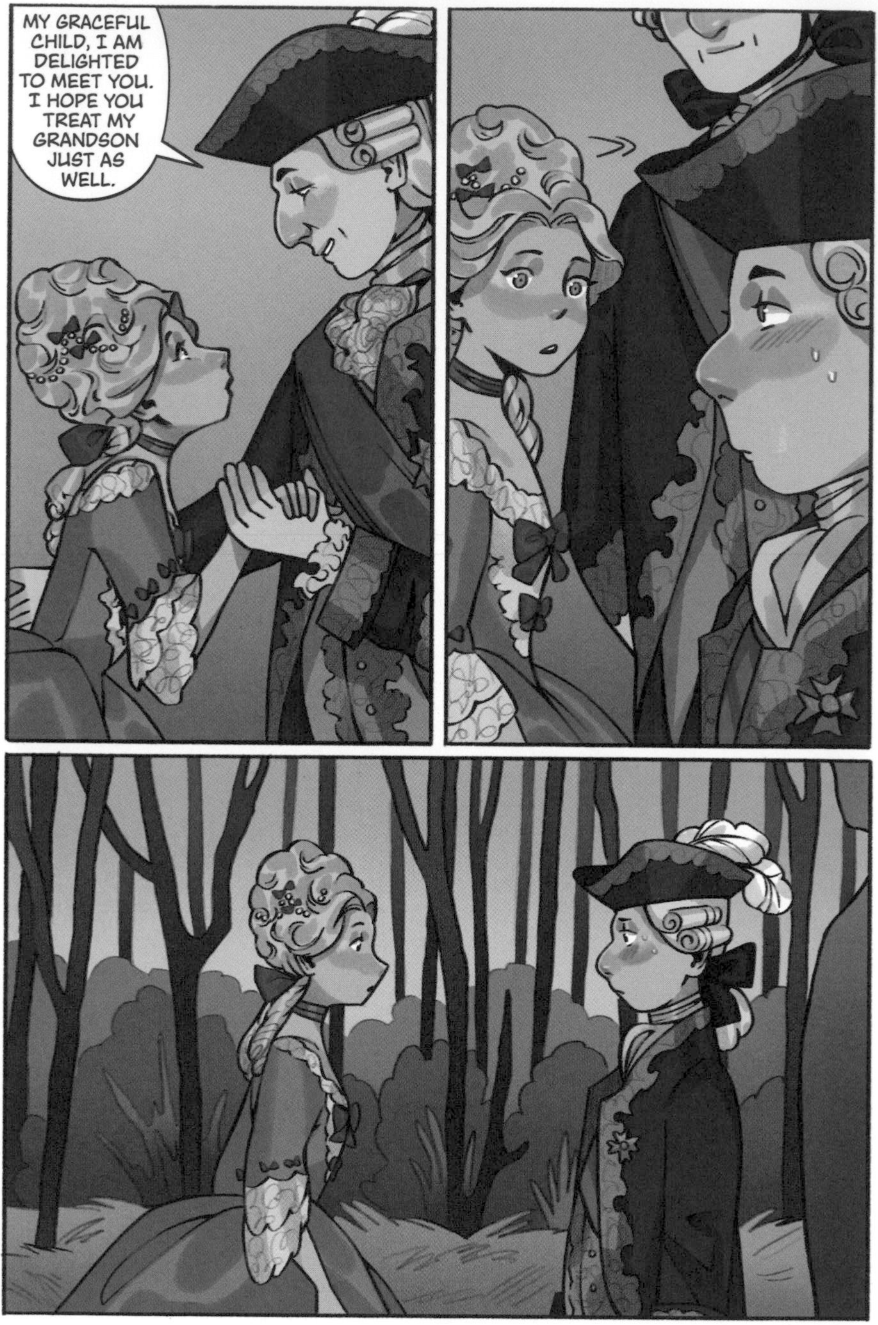
MY GRACEFUL CHILD, I AM DELIGHTED TO MEET YOU. I HOPE YOU TREAT MY GRANDSON JUST AS WELL.

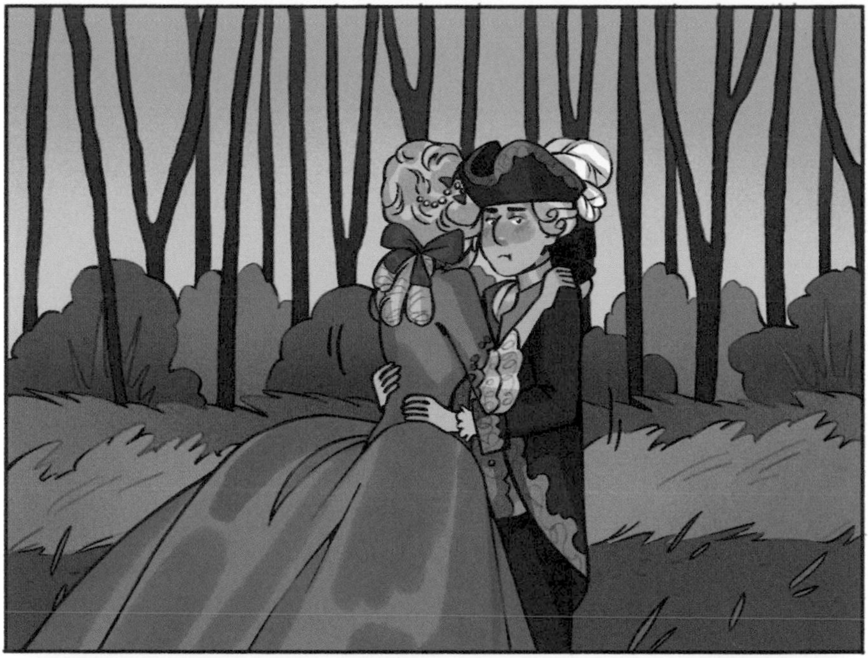

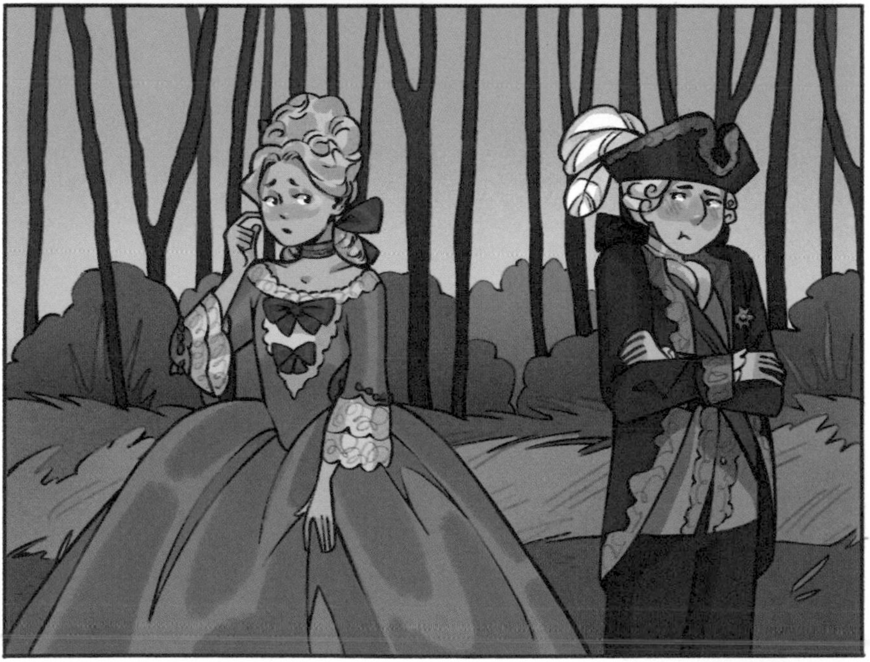

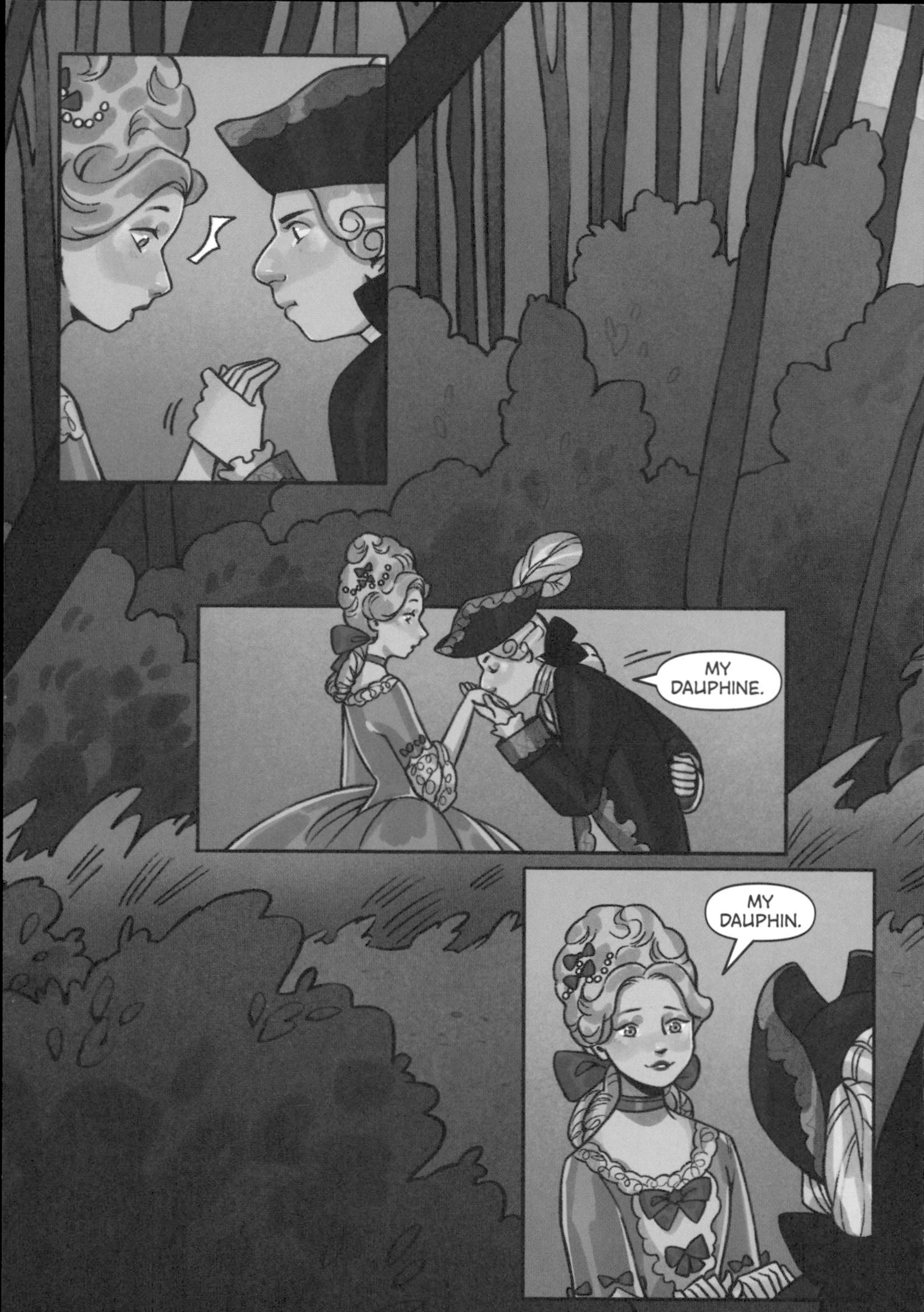
MY DAUPHINE.
MY DAUPHIN.

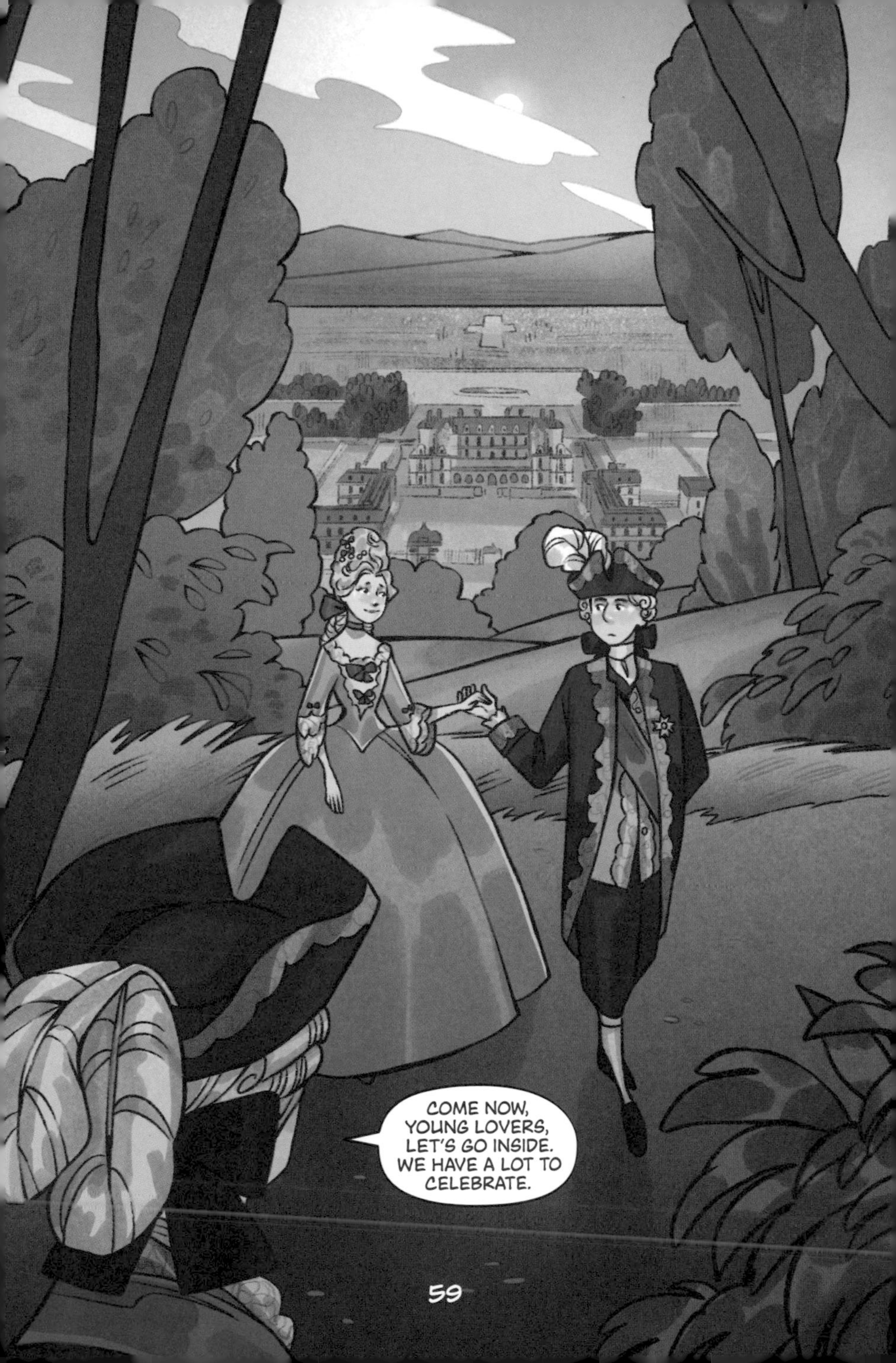
COME NOW, YOUNG LOVERS, LET'S GO INSIDE. WE HAVE A LOT TO CELEBRATE.

Conclusion

After the young Marie Antoinette arrived at Versailles, she struggled for a few years to fit in and create friends. As she and Louis failed to have heirs, pressure and gossip at court grew more intense, especially after the two took the throne. Both still teenagers at the time of King Louis XV's passing, they inherited a country that was struggling financially from the reign of Louis XV and the kings before him. By the time Marie Antoinette had her first child, she was accepted by most of higher society, and even the people of France knew her as someone who loved children and would stop a carriage on the street if she thought a child was hurt.

However, the French people's view of Marie Antoinette changed over the years, especially as the country's economy grew worse and people struggled to make ends meet. Many damaging rumors and scandals arose, including one known as the "Affair of the Diamond Necklace," which led French citizens to believe that the royal court was out of touch with its own people. One of the time's most famous misperceptions is that Marie Antoinette said "Let them eat cake" after hearing that the French people were starving and had no bread; however, this quote has since proven to be falsely attributed to her. These factors were just a few of the pain points that contributed to the public's discontent with the royal family, which ultimately led to Marie Antoinette's and Louis XVI's deaths at the start of the French Revolution. They were the last king and queen of France.

Timeline of Marie Antoinette's Life

1755 — Marie Antoinette is born on November 2

1756 — The Seven Years' War starts on May 17

1763 — The Seven Years' War ends on February 15

1768 — Maria Theresa and Louis XV plan the engagement process for Marie Antoinette and Louis Auguste

1770 — Louis Auguste sends Marie Antoinette a ring declaring their engagement official on January 21

— Their proxy wedding is held in Vienna on April 19

— Marie Antoinette's procession to leave Austria begins on April 21

— The couple meets for the first time on May 14

— Marie Antoinette and Louis Auguste get married at Versailles on May 16

1774 — King Louis XV dies of smallpox on May 10

1775 — Louis Auguste's coronation is held on June 11, making him and Marie Antoinette the king and queen of France

1784 — The "Affair of the Diamond Necklace" incident begins

1789 — The French Revolution starts

1793 — King Louis XVI dies by execution on January 21

— Marie Antoinette dies by execution on October 16

Bibliography

*Books for young readers

Château de Versailles. "Marriage of the Dauphin Louis and Marie Antoinette." Accessed June 10, 2020. https://en.chateauversailles. fr/discover/history/key-dates/marriage-dauphin-louis-and-marie-antoinette.

Fraser, Antonia. **Marie Antoinette**. New York: Anchor Books, 2002.

Lewis, Jone Johnson. "Marie Antoinette Image Gallery." **Thought Co**. Updated March 18, 2017. https://www.thoughtco.com/marie-antoinette-image-gallery-4122972.

*Manzanero, Paula K. **The Who Was? History of the World Deluxe Edition**. New York: Penguin Workshop, 2021.

Mutschlechner, Martin. "Maria Theresa's children." **The World of the Habsburgs**. Accessed June 10, 2020. https://www.habsburger. net/en/chapter/maria-theresas-children.

*Rau, Dana Meachen. **Who Was Marie Antoinette?** New York: Penguin Workshop, 2015.

"Schönbrunn Palace." **Schönbrunn Group: Discover Imperial Austria**. Accessed June 10, 2020. https://www.schoenbrunn-group.com/ en/tourism/schoenbrunn-palace.

Soryo, Fuyumi. **Marie Antoinette: La jeunesse d'une reine**. Tokyo: Kodansha, 2016.

Timms, Elizabeth Jane. "Vienna to Versailles: Inside the bridal procession of Marie Antoinette." **Royal Central**. September 20, 2019. https://royalcentral.co.uk/features/vienna-to-versailles-inside-the-bridal-procession-of-marie-anto inette-130696/.

ABOUT THE CREATORS

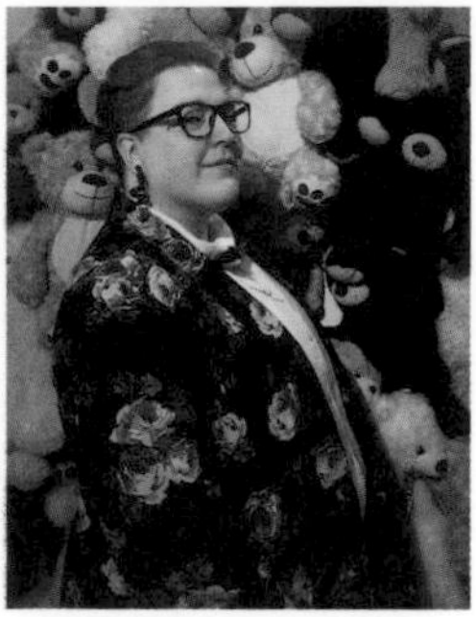
KYLE LEOPARD

Bones Leopard is a twin and nonbinary writer and artist who currently haunts Massachusetts. They wrote *Pandora's Legacy* and *Save Yourself!* for BOOM! Studios. Bones loves all things cats, comics, and cozy. They currently have two cats, Chestah and Callisto, who are no help at all when it comes to work.

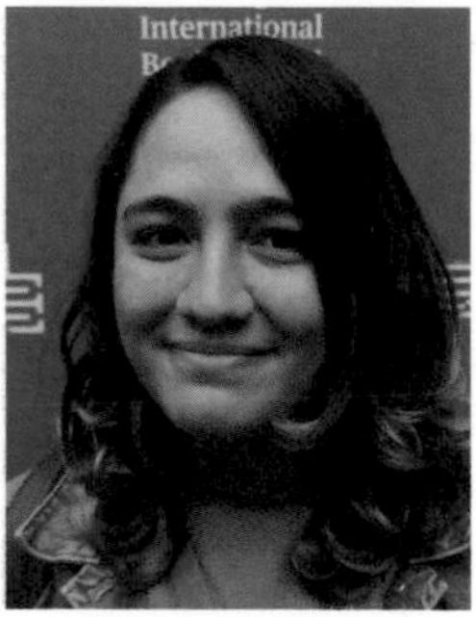
International
KAT HALL

Robin Richardson is a nonbinary Malaysia-based author and illustrator. With the ability to tackle most artistic styles, they enjoy creating work to entice different audiences. They have illustrated for a variety of publishers and clients, including BHP Comics, Z2 Comics, Penguin Random House, and Discord. When they aren't writing or drawing, they're cozied up with a cup of tea, their favorite video games, and their two cats, Scrunkles and Paya.